101 Mix & Match Recipes with Vegetables

By

Satarupa Banerjee

PUSTAK MAHAL®
Delhi • Bangalore • Mumbai • Patna • Hyderabad

Publishers
Pustak Mahal®, Delhi

J-3/16 , Daryaganj, New Delhi-110002
☎ 23276539, 23272783, 23272784 • *Fax:* 011-23260518
E-mail: info@pustakmahal.com • *Website:* www.pustakmahal.com

Sales Centre
10-B, Netaji Subhash Marg, Daryaganj, New Delhi-110002
☎ 23268292, 23268293, 23279900 • *Fax:* 011-23280567
E-mail: rapidexdelhi@indiatimes.com

Branch Offices
Bangalore: ☎ 22234025 • *Telefax:* 22240209
E-mail: pmblr@sancharnet.in • pustak@sancharnet.in
Mumbai: ☎ 22010941
E-mail: rapidex@bom5.vsnl.net.in
Patna: ☎ 3294193 • *Telefax:* 0612-2302719
E-mail: rapidexptn@rediffmail.com
Hyderabad: *Telefax:* 040-24737290
E-mail: pustakmahalhyd@yahoo.co.in

ISBN 978-81-223-0638-5

Edition : 2009

Printed at : Param Offsetters, Okhla, New Delhi-110020

Preface

A lot has been said in recent times about vegetarian diets. Including vegetables in our diet is, of course, extremely beneficial. But this book is not for the strict vegetarians. It is for the diehard carnivores who can mix meat, fish and eggs with assorted vegetables and get the best of the both worlds.

It is my belief that a little animal protein mixed with vegetables makes for a better balanced meal. Generally what happens is that the non-vegetarians tend to neglect vegetables. And this is foolish. It is here that this book comes in. It shows how a judicious combination of vegetables and animal protein produces delicious results.

There are some purely vegetarian recipes, too. The recipes show the wide range vegetables have and how they can be mixed and matched to produce superb culinary creations.

So go ahead and try them all. You won't be disappointed, I promise you.

Bon appetite.

Dedication

To my dearest friend
Dolly Majumdar,
With all my love.

Contents

BORSCH

Ingredients (Serves 4)

- 1 medium beetroot
- 100 gm cabbage
- 100 gm potatoes
- 1 onion
- 2 tbsp butter
- 1 tbsp flour
- 4 cups rich stock—chicken or mutton
- Salt and pepper to taste
- 4 tbsp thick tomato puree
- 1 bay leaf
- 2 tsp vinegar or lime juice
- 1/2 tsp powdered all spice
- 1 tbsp sugar
- 2 tbsp curd
- 4 tbsp finely chopped parsley

Preparation

Cook the unpeeled beetroot till tender. Peel and slice thinly. Shred the cabbage; peel and cut the potatoes in small cubes. Slice the onion. Heat the butter in a saucepan. Saute the vegetables for 2 minutes. Add the flour and cook for another two minutes. Add 1 cup of stock; stir well. When it comes to a boil, add the rest of the stock. Add salt and pepper to taste, tomato puree, bay leaf, vinegar, powdered all spice and sugar. Cover and simmer till the vegetables are done. Serve garnished with the curd and parsley.

Variation: Can be served chilled.

French Country Soup

Ingredients (Serves 4)

- 2 sticks celery
- 1 medium potato
- 1 medium carrot
- 1 large tomato
- 1 medium turnip
- Salt and pepper to taste
- 750 ml mutton or chicken stock
- Bechamel sauce

Bechamel Sauce

- 1 clove
- 1 onion
- 300 ml milk
- 1 bay leaf
- 2 tbsp flour
- 2 tbsp butter
- Salt and white pepper to taste

Preparation

Clean and finely chop all the vegetables. Cook in stock till tender. Blend or pass through a sieve to make a puree.

Bechamel Sauce: Stick the onion with the clove. Add to the milk along with the bay leaves. Bring to a boil. Remove from heat and let it steep for half an hour. Blend together the flour and butter in a saucepan over a low heat. Take off fire. Strain the boiled milk and add a little at a time to the flour and butter mixture. When all the milk has been added, return to heat. Add salt and pepper and cook over a slow fire till the flour is well cooked and the sauce is smooth and glossy. Blend the Bechamel sauce with the puree. Serve hot garnished with a swirl of cream.

Variation: Any vegetable can be pureed and cooked this way—pumpkin, bottle gourd, peas, cauliflower, potato, carrot etc.

Green Coconut and Chicken Soup

Ingredients (Serves 6)

- 250 gm boneless chicken
- 1/2 cup tender coconut meat
- 6 French beans
- 2 stalks lemon grass or 1 tsp grated lime rind
- 2 green chillies
- 5½ cups green coconut water
- 1/2 cup shelled peas
- 1 tbsp refined oil
- 1/2 tsp ginger paste
- 1 tsp sugar
- Salt and white pepper to taste
- Pinch of monosodium glutamate
- 1 tbsp cornflour
- A handful of fresh coriander leaves
- Lime juice to taste
- A few drops of green capsico sauce

Preparation

Cut the boneless chicken pieces in slivers. Top and tail the beans and dice into 2-5 cm pieces. Chop lemon grass and green chillies. Put 5 cups of green coconut water and chicken to boil in a large saucepan. Cover and let simmer after it comes to a boil. Halfway through, add the french beans, peas and coconut meat. Remove when the chicken is done. In another saucepan, heat the oil. Stir fry the ginger paste for half a minute; add green chillies. Stir and add the chicken soup. When it comes to a boil, add the lemon grass or lime rind, soya sauce, sugar, salt, white pepper and monosodium glutamate. Let boil for a couple of minutes. In the meantime, mix the cornflour with the remaining 1/2 cup green coconut water. Boil till the soup thickens a little. Remove and serve in individual bowls. Garnish with chopped coriander leaves, lime juice and green capsico sauce.

Variation: Use other green vegetables like spinach, spring onion or lettuce.

Rich Corn Soup

Ingredients (Serves 8)

- 2 cups corn kernels
- 1 large onion
- 1 capsicum
- 1 stick celery
- 100 gm ham
- 1 large potato
- 1 tbsp butter
- Salt and pepper to taste
- 2 tbsp cornflour
- 500 ml clear chicken stock
- 500 ml milk

Preparation

Cook the corn kernels. Finely chop the onion, capsicum, celery and ham. Grate the potato. Heat the butter in a large saucepan. Add the onion and celery and stir till the onion starts to pick up brown spots. Add the potato, salt, pepper and stock. Stir well and bring to a boil. Cook over medium heat. When the potatoes are almost done, add the capsicum, simmer till the potatoes are very soft. Blend the flour with 1/2 cup of milk and add. Stir until the soup starts to boil. Add the rest of the milk, corn and ham. Simmer for 10 minutes. Check seasoning. Serve very hot accompanied by cheese sticks.

Variation: Vegetarians can omit ham and proceed with the recipe.

Tomato Saar

Tomato Soup–The Indian Way

Ingredients (Serves 8)

- 1 kg tomatoes
- 2 onions (optional)
- 2 coconuts
- 2 tbsp refined oil
- 1 tsp mustard seeds
- 2 green chillies, chopped
- 1 sprig curry leaves
- 1 tbsp sugar
- Salt and pepper to taste

Preparation

Wash and quarter the tomatoes. Finely chop the onions. Boil the tomatoes with the onions, salt and 2 cups of water till very soft. Liquidise and strain. Grate the coconut and extract 1 cup of thick milk and 2 cups of thin milk. Mix the tomato juice and thin coconut milk. Heat the oil in a small saucepan and add the mustard seeds, curry leaves and green chillies. Add to the tomato mixture along with the sugar and pepper. Cook over a medium flame for 10 minutes. Remove from heat and add the thick coconut milk. Taste and adjust seasoning. Garnish with chopped coriander leaves and serve hot.

Rice

Cauliflower Risi Bisi

Ingredients

- 1 cup rice
- 1 tbsp butter or refined oil
- 2 tbsp finely chopped capsicum
- 2 tbsp finely chopped onion
- 2 tbsp finely chopped blanched tomatoes
- Salt and pepper to taste

Sauce

- 1 tbsp refined oil
- 5 green chillies
- 1/3 cup milk
- 1cup cream
- 1 medium cauliflower, divided into florets,
- Refined oil for deep frying

For Batter :

- 125 ml chicken stock
- 4 tbsp flour
- Bread crumbs as needed
- 1/2 tsp salt
- 1/2 tsp ajwain

Preparation

Rice: Cook the rice. Heat the butter or oil in a skillet, saute capsicum, onion and tomatoes for 2 minutes. Add rice and stir to mix well. Season with salt and pepper. Keep warm.

Sauce: Heat the oil in a small frying pan and season with the slit green chillies. When they emit their aroma, remove from oil. Blend with the milk to make a paste. Mix with the beaten cream, salt and pepper. Parboil the cauliflower in lightly salted water. Drain and reserve.

Batter: Mix the flour and stock to a smooth batter. Dip the cauliflower florets in the batter and roll in bread-crumbs seasoned with salt and ajwain. Deep fry in hot oil till golden brown.

To Serve: Prepare a bed of rice on a rice plate. Arrange cauliflowers on it and pour the sauce over.

Garnish with red and green capsicum juliennes.

Polynesian Rice

Ingredients (Serves 6)

- 2 green coconuts
- $1^1/_2$ cups Dehradun rice
- 2 cm piece of ginger
- 4 green chillies
- 1 medium carrot
- 8 french beans
- 1/2 cup shelled peas
- 4 tsp ghee
- 1 tsp cumin seeds
- 1 tsp chilli powder
- 1 tsp garam masala powder
- Salt to taste
- $1^1/_2$ orange juice
- $1^1/_2$ cups green coconut water
- 2 tbsp grated coconut
- 2 tbsp finely chopped fresh coriander

Preparation

Cut the tops of the green coconut. The coconut seller will do this for you. Pour out the water and reserve. Grind the ginger and green chillies together. Peel the carrot and cut into 5 cm long pieces. Top and tail the beans and cut into the same length. Boil all the vegetables for 5 minutes and strain. Wash the rice and soak for half an hour. Heat the ghee in a degchi, temper with the cumin seeds. Add the vegetables. Saute for 5 minutes. Add the strained rice and stir fry till it acquires a parched look. Add the chilli powder, garam masala powder, salt, orange juice and green coconut water. Cover once it comes to a boil and reduce heat. When the moisture reaches the level of the rice and you find holes appearing on a surface, add the ginger-green chilli paste. Fluff up the rice with a light hand and put on dum. This means, putting a tawa underneath the degchi and cooking till the rice is done and fluffy, say for about 20-25 minutes. Fill the two green coconut shells with the rice; garnish each with a tablespoon of grated coconut and fresh coriander.

Variation: Use 1 tablespoon sugar, if the orange juice is sour, other vegetables of your choice can be used as well. You may also add nuts and raisins.

Vangi Bhat

(Brinjal Rice)

An one dish meal–all that is needed to complete the menu is a raita.

Ingredients (Serves 4)

- 2 cups basmati rice
- Salt to taste
- 1 tbsp whole garam masala
- $1^{1}/_{2}$ tsp coriander seeds
- $1^{1}/_{2}$ tsp cumin seeds
- 1 tbsp sesame seeds
- 1 tbsp groundnuts
- 1 coconut
- 8 small brinjals
- 8 small potatoes
- 1 tsp chilli powder
- 3 tbsp refined oil
- 3 tbsp tomato puree
- 4 tbsp cream
- A pinch of saffron (optional)
- 1/2 tsp garam masala powder

Grind together

- 2.5 cm ginger
- 2 cloves garlic
- 4 green chillies

Preparation

Pick, wash and soak the rice for half an hour. Cook rice with enough salted water and the whole garam masala till 3/4 done. Strain and keep aside. Lightly broil the coriander and cumin seeds and grind to a powder. Broil and powder the sesame seeds and groundnuts separately. Grind the coconut with 1 cup of water in the blender and extract 1 cup of milk. Slit the brinjals into quarters, but do not cut through. Parboil, peel and quarter the potatoes likewise. Mix the sesame seed powder, half the coriander-cumin powder, chilli powder and a 1/4 teaspoon of salt together. Stuff the brinjals with this masala. Mix the groundnut powder and the remaining coriander-cumin and chilli powder and salt. Stuff the potatoes with this masala. Heat the oil in a karahi. Add the ground paste and saute for a minute. Add the tomato puree and the stuffed vegetables. Stir carefully, sprinkle 1/4 cup of water. Cover and cook till the

Rich Corn Soup

Meat Balls in Pea Gravy

Maharashtrian Sambhar

Dilpasand Kofta

Potato Dam Pukht

Khatta Meetha Karela

vegetables are done and the moisture evaporated. Grease a baking dish. Divide the rice in three parts. Layer one part of the rice at the bottom. Top with the potatoes. Spread another portion of rice. Layer the brinjals. Cover with the remaining rice. Pour the coconut milk all over. Mix the cream and saffron, if using. Dot over the rice. Sprinkle the garam masala. Bake in an oven preheated to 190°C/380° F for half an hour.

Two in One Ring Pulao

Ingredients (Serves 4)

Rice

- 1 cup basmati rice
- Juice of one lime

Green Layer

- 2 cups chopped spinach
- 2 green chillies
- 1 cm piece of ginger
- 2 cloves garlic
- 2 tbsp ghee
- 1 onion, chopped
- Salt to taste
- 1/2 cup boiled peas
- 1/2 tsp garam masala powder

Orange Layer

- 2 tomatoes
- 1 medium onion
- 2 tbsp ghee
- 1 cup grated carrot
- 1/2 tsp chilli powder
- 1/2 tsp garam masala powder
- Salt to taste
- 1 tsp sugar

For Garnish

- Tomato slices

Preparation

Rice: Parboil the rice in salted water. Drain well and mix the lime juice.

Green layer: Boil spinach with 1 tablespoon of water. Cool and grind alongwith the green chillies, ginger and garlic. Heat the ghee. Fry the onions till soft. Add the spinach and salt and fry, stirring, till the ghee separates. This will take at least 10 minutes. Mix half the rice, peace and garam masala. Remove from heat.

Orange layer: Blanch the tomatoes and blend in the mixie. Strain. Chop the onion. Heat the ghee. Fry the onion till transparent. Add the carrot and fry for 2-3 minutes. Add the tomatoes alongwith the remaining ingredients. Cook till the ghee separates. This takes a little time and patience. Mix with the remaining rice.

The finale: Grease a 16 cm ring mould. Spread the green rice. Press to make an even layer. Then spread the orange rice. Press. Cover with aluminium foil and bake in an oven preheated to 200° C for 20 minutes. Let it cool a little and invert on a serving plate. Garnish with tomato rings.

Variation: Can be steamed in a pressure cooker without the pressure for 10 minutes. A dhokla steamer or rice cooker may also be used. The hollow of the mould can be filled with a salad to make a complete meal. Cooked prawns or boneless chicken cubes may be used for a non-vegetarian version.

Kathal Ki Biriyani

(Jackfruit Biriyani)

Ingredients (Serves 6)

Yakhni

- 1 tsp cumin seeds
- 1 tsp coriander seeds
- 4 bay leaves
- 2 cm piece of ginger
- 1 small piece of dry turmeric
- 4 cloves
- 4 green cardamoms, a few pieces of cinnamon
- 2 whole dry red chillies
- 2 lt of water
- 500 gm basmati rice
- 600 gm raw jackfruit
- Refined oil for frying the jackfruit
- Salt to taste
- 100 gm curd
- 1 tbsp ginger paste
- 1 tsp chilli powder
- 1 tsp cumin powder
- 4 tsp sugar
- 1 tbsp garam masala powder
- 50 gm raisins
- 150 ml ghee
- 25 bay leaves
- 4 black cardamoms
- A pinch of saffron
- 1/2 cup milk
- 1 tbsp kewra water

Preparation

Yakhni: Crush and tie all the spices in a thin muslin cloth. Add to the water and bring to a boil. Cover and simmer till the water is reduced to about $1^1/_2$ lt. Squeeze the muslin to extract maximum flavour and discard. Reserve water. Parboil the rice in the yakhni till 3/4 done. Strain and spread the rice on a tray, keep aside. Peel and discard the middle portion of the jackfruit and cut into thick slices. Parboil and drain. Heat enough oil in a karahi. Smear the jackfruit with a little salt and deep fry till a light brown. Beat the curd and add the ginger paste, chilli powder, cumin powder, 1 teaspoon garam masala powder, sugar, 1 teaspoon salt, and raisins. Soak the fried jackfruit in it for half an hour. Heat half the ghee in a degchi. Add 4 bay leaves and black cardamoms, slightly bruised. When they change colour, add the curd mixture. Wash the vessel with half cup of water and add to it. Cook over a low heat till the jackfruit is tender and a little thick gravy is left.

Finale: Take a heavy bottomed degchi. Cover the bottom with half the bay leaves. Spread 1/3 of the rice over it. Mix the saffron with milk and sprinkle 1 tablespoon over the rice. Top with half the jackfruit alongwith some of the gravy. Likewise, make another layer. Sprinkle the saffron milk over the rice. Cover with the remaining rice and sprinkle the garam masala powder. Heat the rest of the ghee and kewra water and pour over the pulao. Cover with the rest of the bay leaves and put on dum. This means covering the degchi with a tight fitting lid (you may seal with atta dough) and putting over a low heat, keeping a tawa underneath the degchi; keep thus for half an hour. Open the degchi at the time of serving. Discard the topmost bay leaves and serve hot, with a raita and a salad. Goes well with a dry meat preparation or a kabab. Can also be served as an one dish meal.

Variation: May add 50 gm nuts and 50 gm khoya—lightly fried. Do this at the time of layering the rice.

Roti and Breads

Methi Paratha (Fenugreek Paratha)

Ingredients (Makes 8 Parathas)

- 2 green chillies
- 1 cm pieces of ginger
- 2 cups fenugreek leaves
- 1 cup atta
- 1/2 cup bajri ka atta
- 1/2 cup gramflour
- Salt to taste
- 2 tbsp refined oil
- 2 tsp sugar
- 1/2 tsp chilli powder
- 1/4 tsp cumin powder
- A generous pinch of turmeric
- 1 tbsp lime juice
- 1/2 cup curd
- 1/4 tsp garam masala powder
- Refined oil for frying

Preparation

Grind green chillies and ginger together. Wash and squeeze the fenugreek leaves well. Sieve the three types of flour together with the salt. Rub in the 2 tablespoon of refined oil. Mix all the above ingredients except the oil for frying, together into a semi-soft dough. Keep aside for 15 minutes. Divide dough into 8 portions. Roll into thick chappatis with the help of a little dry atta. Heat a tawa. Roast the parathas very lightly on both the sides, then smear with oil and fry till golden brown. Serve with a dry sabji and pickle.

Variation: If you can't get bajri ka atta, add 1/2 cup more atta instead.

MOOLI KA PARATHA (RADISH PARATHA)

Ingredients (Makes 6 Parathas)

For Dough

- $1^3/_4$ cup atta
- 1/2 tsp salt
- 1 tbsp refined oil
- Oil for frying paratha

For Filling

- 3 cups grated radish
- 3 tbsp refined oil
- 2 bay leaves
- 1/4 tsp cumin seeds
- 1/4 tsp rai
- Pinch of asafoetida
- 1/4 tsp ajwain
- Salt to taste
- 1/2 tsp amchur
- 1/2 tsp chilli powder
- 1/2 tsp garam masala powder
- 1/4 tsp grated ginger
- 2 green chillies, finely chopped
- 2 tbsp chopped fresh coriander

Preparation

Dough: Sieve the atta and salt together. Rub in 1 tablespoon oil and make a semi hard dough with water. Knead well. Divide into 6 parts.

Filling: Squeeze the grated radish and get rid of some of the water. Heat the oil in a karahi. Temper with the bay leaves, cumin, rai, ajwain and asafoetida. When the spices stop spluttering, add the radish and the remaining ingredients. Fry well over a medium heat till the water dries up. Divide into 6 parts.

Finale: Take one part of the dough and roll into a small puri. Place one portion of the filling in the centre and roll into a ball again. Roll into a thick chappati with the help of a little dry atta. Roast on a hot tawa. Prick both the sides with a fork at a few places. Then smear the parathas with 1 teaspoon oil and drizzle oil from the sides. Fry both the sides till golden brown. Serve with pickle and raita.

Minty Vegetable Paratha

Ingredients (Makes 8 Parathas)

For Dough

- 2 cups atta
- Salt to taste
- 2 tbsp refined oil
- Oil or ghee for frying

Grind to a paste

- $1\frac{1}{2}$ cup mint leaves
- 1/2 cup fresh coriander
- 2 green chillies

For Stuffing

- 3/4 cup grated carrot
- 3/4 cup shredded cabbage
- 1 small capsicum, finely chopped
- 3 medium potatoes
- 1 tsp amchur powder
- 1 tsp garam masala powder
- 1 tsp roasted and powdered cumin seeds
- Salt to taste

Preparation

Sieve the atta and oil together. Mix the oil and prepare a semi-soft dough with water as needed. Divide into 8 parts and keep aside. Apply 1 teaspoon salt to the carrot, cabbage and capsicum. Leave aside for 1/2 an hour. Squeeze the water very well. There should be no moisture left. Mix the remaining ingredients along with the paste (in case there is any water in the paste, strain). Divide the stuffing into 8 parts. Roll a portion on the dough into a thin chappati. Spread one part of the stuffing over half the chappati. Cover with the other half. It will give the paratha a half moon shape. Flute the edges with the tines of a fork. This serves to secure the edges as well as give the paratha a decorative look. Roast on a hot tawa; then sprinkle oil or ghee from the sides and fry till golden brown.

Variation: Divide the dough into 16 parts. Roll each into a square-shaped paratha. Place a portion of the stuffing on one and cover with another. Seal the edges and fry.

PALAK PANEER PARATHA

Ingredients (Makes 8 Parathas)

For Dough

- 300 gm spinach, leaves only
- 1 cup flour
- 1 cup atta
- Salt to taste
- 2 tbsp melted ghee

For Filling

- 100 gm paneer
- 1 cup cauliflower florets
- 1 large onion
- 1/4 cup fresh coriander
- 4 green chillies or to taste
- Salt to taste
- 1/2 tsp grated ginger
- 1 tsp garam masala powder
- 1 tsp amchur powder

Preparation

Cook the spinach leaves with a pinch each of salt and sugar for just 2 minutes. Do not overcook. Press to get rid of any moisture. Blend to form a puree. Sieve the flour, atta and salt together. Rub in the ghee (use oil in winter). The mixture should resemble bread crumbs. Stir in the blended spinach and knead into a soft dough. If needed, use the water from the cooked spinach.

Filling: Grate the paneer, cauliflower florets and onion. Finely chop the coriander and green chillies. Mix all. Mix 1/2 teaspoon salt with the vegetables and leave aside for half an hour. Squeeze well to get rid of all moisture. Mix the remaining ingredients. Divide both the dough and the filling into 8 parts. Dredge one part of the dough with a little atta and make a large round chappati. Spread one part of the filling over one half of the chappati and cover with the other half. This will give the paratha a half moon shape. Press the edges with the tines of a fork. This secures the edges as well as gives a decorative look. Roast on a hot tawa then fry to a golden brown sprinkling ghee.

Variation: Mix sesame seeds, kalonji and ajwain and press a little of this mixture on one side of the paratha, before frying. Gives an unusual spicy taste.

STUFFED BAKED PURI

Ingredients (Makes 6 Puris)

For Dough

- 1/2 tbsp fresh yeast
- 1/2 tsp sugar
- 1/2 cup warm water
- 1 cup flour
- 1/2 tsp salt
- 1 tbsp refined oil

For Filling

- 1 medium carrot
- 8 French beans
- 1 onion
- 1 small capsicum
- 1 medium potato
- 2 tbsp refined oil
- $1\frac{1}{2}$ tsp pau bhaji masala powder
- $1\frac{1}{2}$ tsp amchur powder
- Salt to taste
- 1 tsp ginger-green chilli paste

Preparation

Mix the yeast, sugar and water in a bowl. Sprinkle 1 teaspoon of flour on top. Cover and keep in a warm place for 5 minutes. Mix salt and oil with the flour. Make a well in the centre and pour in the yeast mixture. Make a soft dough and keep covered, in a warm place for 2 hours or till it doubles in size.

Filling: Chop the carrots, French beans, onion and capsicum finely. Boil and mash the potato. Boil the carrot and beans too. Heat the oil in a karahi. Fry the onion till soft. Add the capsicum. Stir fry. Add the pau bhaji masala and fry. Add the rest of the vegetables along with the other ingredients. Mix well and remove. Divide into 6 parts.

Knock back the dough, that is, punch it down to expel all the air in it. Knead well till smooth and elastic. This will take at least 10 minutes. Divide the dough into 6 parts. Roll each part into a ball and dredge with a little flour and pat into a circle. Stuff each with one part of the filling and roll into a ball again. Roll into a thick puri. Prepare all the puris likewise. Leave in a warm place for 15 minutes. Place on a greased baking tray and bake at 200°C/400°F for 15-20 minutes. Apply butter on top and serve.

Masala Bread

Ingredients (Makes 1 loaf)

For Bread

- 15 gm fresh yeast (1 lemon sized ball approximately)
- 2 tsp sugar
- 3 cup lukewarm milk
- 2 cups flour
- 1 tsp salt
- 2 tbsp refined oil or butter

For Masala

- 1 tbsp refined oil
- 1/4 cup onion
- 1/4 cup carrot
- 1/4 cup capsicum
- 1 tsp green chilli, chopped
- Salt to taste
- Pinch of ajinomoto (optional)

Preparation

Mix the fresh yeast with the sugar and lukewarm milk. Sprinkle 1 tablepsoon flour on top. Keep aside for 10 minutes. Finely chop all the vegetables. Heat the oil in a karahi. Add the onion. Stir fry till transparent. Add the vegetables. Saute for 2 minutes. Add the salt and ajinomoto, if using. Mix well and remove. Mix the flour with salt and oil. Next add the prepared masala to it. Make a bay in the centre. Pour in the yeast mixture and form a soft dough. Cover with cellophane paper and keep in a warm area for 45-50 minutes or till the dough doubles in bulk. It will take longer in winter. Knock back the dough and knead well. Shape into a loaf and put into a greased loaf tin. Keep aside for approximately 20-25 minutes or till it doubles it in volume again. Bake in a preheated oven at 350°F/180°C for 30 minutes.

Variation: Prepare small buns instead of one loaf. You may add chilli powder, roasted cumin powder and chaat masala 1/2 teaspoon each to the vegetables along with salt.

Vegetable with a Non-Vegetarian Ingredient

Egg Florentine

Ingredients (Serves 4)

- 4 eggs
- 1 large bunch spinach
- 2 green chillies
- 1 onion
- 1 tsp finely chopped garlic
- 1 tbsp refined oil
- Salt and pepper to taste
- 1/4 cup grated cheese

For Cheese sauce

- 1 tbsp butter
- 1 tbps flour
- 2 cups milk
- 1 egg yolk
- 1/4 cup cream
- 1/4 cup grated cheese
- Salt and pepper to taste

Preparation

Hard boil the eggs and halve vertically. Wash well and chop the leaves of the spinach, discarding tough stems and bruised leaves. Chop the green chillies and onion. Heat the oil in a skillet. Add the garlic. Saute till the raw smell disappears. Add the onion and green chillies and stir fry till the onion softens. Add the chopped spinach and salt. Bring to a boil, reduce heat and cook till the spinach is done. Keep aside. Melt the butter in a saucepan. Add the flour; blend well. Reduce heat and add the milk, a little at a time, stirring well till all the milk is used. There should be no lumps. Simmer till the flour is cooked and the sauce looks glossy. Beat the egg yolk and cream together. Stir in a spoonful of the hot sauce. Mix well and then add to the sauce. Add half the grated cheese. Remove.

To Serve: Take a greased baking dish, spread the spinach. Place the halved eggs on it. Pour the cheese sauce on top. Sprinkle the grated cheese. Bake in an oven preheated to 350°F/170°C for 20 minutes. Serve at once.

Variation: Sauteed fish fillet can be baked the same way.

Roasted Chicken With Vegetable Stuffing

Ingredients (Serves 6)

Chicken

- 1 chicken, approx 1-1$^1/_2$ kg
- 2 tbps ground raw papaya
- 1 tbsp salt
- 200 ml curd
- 1 tbsp Kashmiri chilli powder
- 1$^1/_2$ tbsp butter

Grind together

- 6 cloves of garlic
- 5 cm piece of ginger
- 2 green chillies

For Garnish

- Shredded lettuce and grated carrots

For Stuffing

- 2 medium carrots
- 1 medium potato
- 8-10 French beans
- 1/3 cup shelled peas
- 10 cashewnuts
- 15 raisins
- 3 tbsp flour
- 1/2 cup milk
- Salt to taste
- 200 ml cream
- 2 tsp mustard paste

Preparation

Remove the skin and keep the chicken whole. Wash well and dry. Make small slits with a knife all over. Mix the papaya paste, salt and ground masala. Rub the spice mixture all over the chicken and marinate for 4 hours. Beat the curd with the kashmiri chilli powder. Steep the chicken in it for half an hour before cooking. Boil the vegetables; peel and cut into small cubes. Mix the flour with the milk. Add the vegetables, cashewnuts, raisins, cream, a little salt and mustard powder. Stuff the chicken with half the vegetable mixture. Sew up the opening. Grease a large baking dish. Put the chicken in the middle and brush with the butter. Bake in an oven preheated to 190°C/380°F for approx. 1 hour or till the chicken is done. Half way through the baking time spread the remaining vegetable mixture around the chicken. Serve on a platter surrounded with shredded lettuce and grated carrots.

Saffron Chicken Casserole

Ingredients (Serves 4)

- 125 gm small onions
- 8-10 button mushrooms
- 2 stalks celery
- 2 large capsicums
- 1 cup flour
- 8 chicken drumsticks
- A generous pinch of saffron
- 1 cup chicken stock
- Salt and pepper to taste
- 1 cup cream
- 1 tbsp butter
- 1 tbsp flour
- Refined oil for frying the chicken

Preparation

Peel, but keep the onions whole. Slice the mushrooms; chop the celery. Discard the seeds and chop capsicums. Place the flour in a paper bag and place 2 chicken drumsticks at a time. Close bag and shake till the chicken pieces are well coated with flour. Repeat with the rest. Heat the oil in a karahi and fry the chicken till brown on all sides. You'll have to do it in 2 batches. Take out and place the chicken at the bottom of a casserole. Saute the onion and mushrooms in 2 tablespoon oil. Remove and spread over the chicken. Saute the capsicum separately in 1 tablespoon oil. Dilute the saffron in 2 tablespoon warm milk and add to the capsicum. Pour in the stock and bring to a boil. Reduce heat and cook for 2 minutes. Remove from fire and stir in the cream. Pour over the chicken. Cover and bake in an oven preheated to 350°F/180°C for 25-30 minutes. Remove the chicken and vegetables into a hot serving dish. Heat the butter in a small frying pan and stir in the flour. Gradually pour in the liquid from the casserole. Cook over a low heat. When it thickens pour over the chicken and vegetables and serve hot.

Variation: A whole chicken, cut into regular pieces may be used. Try to use one red and one green capsicum. It adds to the colour and beauty.

Moussaka Orangello

Adaptation of the famous mediterranean dish

Ingredients (Serves 6)

- 500 gm brinjals, long variety preferred
- 2 large onions
- Refined oil for frying

For Mince

- 1 large onion
- 2 cloves garlic
- 1 large capsicum
- 6 button mushrooms
- 10 prawns
- 1/3 cup shelled peas
- 2 tbsp flour
- 1/2 kg minced mutton
- 1 cup chicken stock
- 2 cups fresh orange juice
- 2 tbsp tomato ketchup
- 1 tsp sugar
- Salt and pepper to taste
- 4 cubes cheese, grated
- 1 egg yolk
- 4 tbsp cream

Preparation

Slice the brinjals and onions into 1 cm thick roundels. Fry the brinjals and onions separately in refined oil till just softened. You'll have to do this in batches. Remove and keep aside. Chop the onion and garlic for the mince. Deseed and chop the capsicum. Slice the mushrooms. Shell and devein the prawns. Remove four for decoration. Boil these. Chop the rest. Parboil the mushroom and peas. Heat 1 tablespoon oil in a saucepan. Saute the onion and garlic till soft and translucent. Add the flour and fry for another minute. Add the mince, capsicum, mushroom, peas and prawn; keep on stirring for 2 minutes. Mix together the stock, orange juice, tomato ketchup and sugar and pour on the mince. Season with salt and pepper. Simmer uncovered for 10 minutes or till the whole mixture is thick. Lightly grease a 20 cm baking dish and line with alternate layers of brinjal, mince, sauteed onion and cheese, retaining half the cheese, beginning and ending with brinjals. Bake in an oven preheated to 350°F/170°C for 35-40 minutes. Mix the egg yolk with the cream. Pour on the brinjals and sprinkle the rest of the grated cheese on top. Return to the oven for 5-10 minutes. Garnish with the boiled prawns and serve hot.

Variation: May omit the prawns.

Prawns with Beetroot

Ingredients (Serves 6)

- 500 gm prawns
- 2 medium beetroots
- 2 medium potatoes
- 1 large onion
- 4 green chillies
- 1/4 cup mustard oil
- 1 tsp finely chopped garlic
- 1 tbsp grated ginger
- Pinch to turmeric
- 1 tsp chilli powder
- 1 tsp sugar
- Salt to taste

Preparation

Shell and devein the prawns. Wash, peel and slice the beetroots, potatoes and onion into thin slices. Then halve to look like half moon shapes. Slit the green chillies. Heat the oil till it smokes to get rid of its pungency. Season with garlic. Fry till the garlic changes colour; add the ginger and green chillies. Fry for another minute. Add the onions and saute till soft, but do not brown. Put in the potatoes, beetroot, turmeric, chilli powder, sugar, salt and prawns. Stir fry for a couple of minutes. Cover and cook over a low heat till done. There is no need to add water. The beetroot will remain crisp, yet tender. Stir continually. The consistency of the gravy should be thick. It is sweet in taste and red in colour. Goes exceptionally well with boiled rice. If you want the curry to look richer, add 1 tablespoon Kashmiri chilli powder in place of the ordinary chilli powder.

Parwal Dolma (Stuffed Parwal)

Ingredients (Serves 6)

- 12 large parwals
- Mustard oil for frying

Filling

- 1/2 kg fish
- 1 large onion
- 6 cashewnuts
- 15 raisins
- 2 cm piece of ginger
- 2 tbps mustard oil
- 1 tbsp chilli powder
- 1/2 tsp turmeric
- 1 tsp sugar
- Salt to taste
- 1/2 tsp garam masala powder

Preparation

Wash and peel the parwals. Make a slit in the middle and carefully take out the seeds. Any large fish like rohu, katla or bhetki will do for the filling. Steam fish. Debone. Finely chop the onion. Chop the cashewnuts into small pieces. Wash raisins. Grate ginger. Heat the oil in a karahi. Add the onion and fry till light brown. Add all the remaining ingredients and fry till the oil separates. Divide into 12 portions. Take each parwal and stuff one portion of the filling. Tie each with a thread. Heat enough oil in a karahi for deep frying. Fry the parwals—4 at a time, till done, Parwals should never be overfried. They are done once they soften. Remove the thread before serving.

Canneloni

Ingredients (Serves 4)

For Pancakes

- 1 cup flour
- Pinch of salt
- $1^1/_2$ tsp refined oil
- 1 egg
- $1^1/_4$ cup milk

For Stuffing

- 200 gm paneer, grated
- 2 green chillies, chopped
- 1 bunch spinach
- Pinch of nutmeg powder
- 3 tbsp thick white sauce
- Salt to taste
- A dash of Worcestershire sauce

For Topping

- 3 teacups white sauce
- 3 tbsp grated cheese

Preparation

Pancakes: Sift the flour and salt together. Make a well in the centre. Add the oil and break the egg into it. Gradually add the milk and mix to make a smooth batter. Cover, and keep aside for half an hour. Heat a small pan. Brush with a little oil and pour a ladleful of batter. Cook over moderate heat until the underside is light brown. Flip over and cook the other side. Cook the rest of the batter the same way.

Stuffing: Boil the spinach in water for 2 minutes. Drain and plunge it in cold water. This helps to retain the colour. Squeeze the spinach to take out all the water. Chop finely. Mix the chopped spinach with paneer, chillies, salt nutmeg, white sauce and Worcestershire sauce. Fill each pancake with the stuffing and roll up. Grease a 16 cm baking dish and arrange the pancakes. Pour the white sauce and top with the cheese. Bake in an oven preheated to 375°F/190°C for 10-15 minutes. Garnish with tomatoes and serve hot.

Kuku Paka

An African dish, adapted to suit Indian taste

Ingredients (Serves 4)

- $1\frac{1}{2}$ coconuts
- 4 cups of water
- 1 small chicken
- 3 medium tomatoes
- 4 green chillies
- 1 large onion
- 4 medium potatoes
- 1 cup corn kernels
- 2 eggs
- 1 tbsp refined oil
- 2 tsp coriander powder
- 1 tsp cumin powder
- Salt to taste
- 1 tsp white pepper
- 1 tsp sugar
- Chopped fresh coriander

Preparation

Grate the coconut. Extract the milk using 2 cups of water. Have the chicken cut in small pieces. Chop the tomatoes and green chillies. Chop the onion finely. Boil the potatoes, corn kernels and eggs. Peel and dice two potatoes; mash the other two. Pressure cook the chicken, tomatoes and green chillies with 1/2 cup of coconut milk. Remove chicken when done. Blend and strain the stock and keep aside. Heat the oil. Add onion and saute till soft, but do not brown. Add the coriander-cumin powder, saute for 1/2 minute and add the coconut milk. Allow to boil while stirring all the time. Add the chicken, mashed potatoes, stock, salt, white pepper and sugar. Mix well. Add the diced potatoes, corn kernels and cook. Stir continually till thick. Remove. Serve sprinkled with fresh coriander and garnished with sliced hard boiled eggs.

Khorme Sabzi (Mutton and Vegetable Curry)

Ingredients (Serves 4)

- 1 bunch dill leaves
- 1 bunch fresh coriander
- 1 bunch fenugreek leaves
- 2 bunches spinach
- 3 medium potatoes
- 3 knol khols (ganth gobi)
- 2 onions
- 2 tomatoes
- 1/2 kg mutton
- 1 heaped tsp ginger-garlic paste
- 1 tsp chilli powder
- Salt to taste
- 2 tbsp refined oil
- 5 cm piece of cinnamon
- 2 cloves
- 2 tsp coriander powder
- 1 tsp amchur powder

Preparation

Clean and shop the greens finely. Peel and quarter the potatoes and knol khols. Slice the onions and chop the tomatoes. Pressure cook the mutton alongwith the potatoes, khol khols, tomatoes, ginger-garlic paste, chilli powder, salt, half the onions and 3 cups of water for 15 minutes. Heat the oil in a degchi. Season with the coarsely powdered cinnamon and cloves. Add the rest of the onions and fry till a light brown. Add the coriander powder. Stir fry for 1 minute. Add the chopped greens and fry over high heat till the moisture evaporates. Stir in the mutton and gravy and cook over a medium heat till the greens are thoroughly cooked. Lastly, add the amchur powder. Mix. The gravy should be thick. Serve hot with chappatis and parathas.

Variation: Can be made without mutton by adding more potatoes and knol khols.

Meat Balls in Pea Gravy

Ingredients (Serves 6)

For Meat Balls

- 250 gm minced mutton
- 50 gm gram dal
- 1 tsp grated ginger
- 1 tsp chilli powder
- Salt to taste
- 1 egg
- 1 tsp lime juice
- Refined oil for frying

For Gravy

- 2 large onions
- 2 cups shelled peas
- 2 tbsp refined oil
- 1 tsp ginger paste
- 1 tsp garlic paste
- 1 tsp coriander powder
- 1 tsp chilli powder
- 1 tbsp poppy seed paste
- Salt to taste
- 1/2 cup tomato puree
- 1/2 cup cream

Preparation

Meatballs: Pressure cook minced meat, gram dal, grated ginger and salt together with very little water for 10 minutes. Dry excess liquid, if any. Grind the cooked mince to a smooth paste. Add chilli powder, egg and lime juice. Form into small balls and deep fry till golden.

Gravy: Finely chop the onions. Boil the peas. Heat the oil in a karahi. Add the onion and fry till soft. Add the ginger garlic paste, coriander and chilli powders and poppy seed paste one after the other, stir frying after each addition. Fry till you find specks of oil appearing over the surface. Add the boiled peas, 2 cups of water, salt and tomato puree. Cover and simmer for 10 minutes. Let it cool a little. Blend the gravy and strain. Put on a low heat again. Add water if its too thick. Put in the koftas and let it boil for 5 minutes on medium heat. Lower heat. Stir in the cream, cook for 2-3 minutes. Serve with naans, parathas or pulaos.

Variations: Any other kofta–like malai kofta, fish kofta, prawn balls can be cooked the same way.

Bottle Gourd and Mutton Stew

Ingredients (Serves 4)

- 500 gm bottle gourd
- 1 large onion
- 1/2 kg mutton
- Salt and pepper to taste
- 2 tbsp ghee or oil
- 6 cloves
- 5 cm stick of cinnamon
- 4 green cardamoms
- 2 bay leaves
- 1/2 cup curd
- 1 cup thick coconut milk
- A handful of chopped fresh coriander

Grind to a paste

- 2.5 cm piece of ginger
- 4 cloves garlic
- 2 green chillies

Preparation

Peel and cut the bottle gourd into cubes. Slice the onion. Cook the mutton in a pressure cooker with the ground masala, salt and 2 cups of water for 15 minutes. Heat the ghee or oil in a degchi. Temper with the cloves, cinnamon, green cardamoms and bay leaves, slightly crushed. When they turn a shade darker, add the onion. When the onions start to pick up brown spots, add the gourd and stir for a minute. Add 1/2 cup of water, a little salt and cook, with lid on till 3/4 done. Transfer the gourd to the meat along with any accumulated juice. Cover and cook till the gourds are well done. Add a little hot water, if necessary. Beat the curd and add to the coconut milk. Reduce heat and add this to the mutton. Keep stirring well. Simmer covered for 5 minutes. Remove and serve sprinkled with pepper and chopped green coriander. This is generally served at room temperature. Has a very cooling effect on the body; extremely suitable dish for summer.

Variation: Papaya, squash, tinda, white pumpkin may be cooked the same way. Or, a mixed stew can be prepared with these vegetables.

Kamalkakri and Keema (Lotus Stem and Minced Meat)

Ingredients (Serves 6)

- 2 large onions
- 1/2 kg kamalkakri
- 3 large tomatoes
- 2 cm piece of ginger
- 4 tbsp ghee
- 1/2 kg minced mutton
- 4 green chillis
- Salt to taste
- A pinch of sodium bicarbonate
- 1 tbsp coriander powder
- 1 tsp turmeric powder
- 1 tsp chilli powder
- A handful of chopped coriander leaves

Preparation

Slice the onions, chop green chillies and tomatoes. Peel and cut the kamalkakri into 1 cm slices and wash well. Grind the ginger. Heat 2 tablespoon ghee in a degchi and fry the onions till brown. Put in the mince; add green chillies and salt. Cook, stirring well. The mince will release its own water. Cook over a medium heat, stirring continually till the water dries up. Remove. In another degchi, heat the remaining 2 tablespoon ghee and add the kamalkakri, salt (remember the mince is already salted) and soda; fry for a few minutes. Add 1 1/2 cups of hot water. Cook uncovered over a high heat. When the water dries, add the kamalkakri. Stir. Add the tomatoes, coriander powder, turmeric, chilli and ginger paste. Keep on stirring for a while. Add 1 1/2 cups of hot water. Simmer covered, over a low heat till the gravy is reduced considerably. Sprinkle the coriander leaves on top and cook for another 5 minutes. Can be served as a snack or with rice and dal.

Variation: The stuffed parwals can be curried in gravy. Minced mutton or prawns can replace fish. Vegetarians can use paneer.

Baghare Baigan (Spicy Brinjal)

Ingredients (Serves 6)

- 12 small round brinjals
- 1/3 cup refined oil for frying the brinjals
- 3 tbsp coriander seeds
- 4 dry red chillies
- 3 large onions
- 4 green chillies
- 1/2 coconut
- 2 tbsp sesame seeds
- 2 tbsp poppy seeds
- 2 tbsp refined oil
- 1 tsp turmeric
- 1/4 cup thick tamarind pulp
- Salt to taste
- 1 tbsp powder jaggery

For Tadka

- 2 tbsp ghee
- 1 tsp mustard seeds, a sprig of curry leaves
- 1/2 tsp chilli powder

Preparation

Wash and slit the brinjals lengthwise into four, but keep the stems intact. In 1 teaspoon of oil fry the coriander seeds and red chillies and grind alongwith 2 onions, green chillies and coconut. Roast the remaining onion over a flame till the onion skins get charred. Cool and wash off the blackened skin. Grind to pulp. Roast the sesame seeds and poppy seeds separately, till you get a fried aroma and grind to a powder. Heat the oil in a karahi. Add the brinjals and fry till the skins get a brownish tinge. Remove. Heat 2 tablespoon oil in the same karahi and fry the ground masala, turmeric and the roasted onion paste over a moderate heat till the oil floats on top. Mix the tamarind pulp with 4 cups of water and add to the masala. When it comes to a boil, add the brinjals and the powdered sesame and poppy seeds, salt and jaggery. Cover and cook till the gravy thickens considerably. *Tadka:* Heat the ghee, temper with the mustard seeds. When they splutter, add the curry leaves and chilli powder. Pour over the curry and serve hot.

Tinde ka Dum

Ingredients (Serves 4)

- 8 large, but tender tindas
- Refined oil for frying
- Salt to taste

For Filling

- 2 cups shelled peas
- 1 tbsp refined oil
- 1/2 tsp whole cumin seeds
- A pinch of asafoetida
- 1 tsp coriander powder
- Salt to taste
- 1/2 tsp turmeric powder
- 1 tsp grated ginger
- 4 finely chopped green chillies
- 4 tbsp grated coconut
- 1/3 cup chopped fresh coriander leaves
- $1^1/_2$ tsp sugar

For Garnish

- 6 cashewnuts, chopped
- 2 sheets silver foil

Preparation

Peel the tindas and cut off a thin slice from the stalk end. Scoop out the seeds. Heat enough oil in a karahi. Smear the tindas with a little salt and deep fry the tindas lightly for 2-3 minutes over a high heat. Take out and keep inverted on a plate.

Filling: Boil the peas. Heat the oil in a karahi. Temper with the cumin seeds and asafoetida. Add the boiled peas, coriander powder, salt, turmeric, ginger and green chillies. Stir and keep on pressing the peas with the ladle so they get somewhat mashed. Stir fry over a medium heat for 3 minutes. Add the coconut, fresh coriander, sugar and fry for another 2 minutes. Remove. When cool enough to handle, fill the tindas with the pea mixture. Press to fill the cavity well. Take a skillet, non-stick preferred. Put the remaining filling, half cup of water and the stuffed tindas. Cover and cook over a low heat, till the tindas are done and the moisture evaporated. You may finish in an oven or tandoor also. Garnish with chopped cashewnuts and silver warq.

Variation: Small brinjals can, very successfully, be cooked this way.

SABZ KHADA MASALA
(VEGETABLES WITH WHOLE SPICES)

Ingredients (Serves 6)

- 2 small onions
- 1 large tomato
- 8 French beans
- 1 medium carrot
- 1 medium potato
- 4 large cauliflower florets
- 1/2 cup shelled peas
- 2 bay leaves
- 5 cm stick of cinnamon
- 1 blade of mace
- 4 cloves
- 4 green cardamoms
- 5 whole red chillies
- 50 gm ghee
- 1 tsp grated ginger
- 1 tsp chopped garlic
- Salt to taste
- 1/2 tsp turmeric powder
- 1 tsp chilli powder
- 1 tbsp thick curd
- 4 green chillies
- 1 tsp garam masala powder

For Garnishi

- 1/2 cup cream
- Fresh coriander
- Green chillies

Preparation

Finely chop the onions and tomato. Cut the vegetables into small pieces. Heat the ghee and temper with the whole spices–bay leaves, cinnamon, mace, cloves, cardamoms and chillies. When these turn a shade darker, add the onions and cook till soft. Add ginger and garlic. Saute till the raw smell of the garlic disappears. Add all the vegetables. Stir well. Add salt, turmeric, chilli powder and saute. Cover and cook for a while, adding 1/4 cup of water. When the vegetables are almost done, add the whipped curd, garam masala powder and chopped green chillies. Cook till the vegetables are tender. Do not add more water. Cover and cook covered on a low heat. The vegetables will cook in their own juices. Lastly, add the cream and remove. Garnish with fresh coriander and slit green chillies.

Mochar Ghonto (Banana Flower Medley)

Ingredients (Serves 6)

- 100 gm urad dal
- 6 whole peppercorns
- 1 tsp coriander seeds
- 1 tsp cumin seeds
- A pinch of asafoetida
- Salt to taste
- Mustard oil as required
- 1 medium banana flower
- 2 cups milk
- 1 tsp cumin powder
- 1/2 tsp pepper powder
- 2 tbsp sugar
- 2 dry red chillies
- 2 bay leaves
- Grated coconut for garnishing

Preparation

Soak the urad dal overnight. Drain and grind with coarsely pounded peppercorns, coriander and cumin seeds. Also add the asafoetida and a pinch of salt. Beat till fluffy. Heat enough oil in a karahi for deep frying. Drop spoonfuls of the dal mixture into the hot oil and fry till golden brown. Set aside. Wash the chopped banana flowers well. Boil in fresh water and strain. Roughly mash the cooked flower with your hands. Mix with the milk, cumin and pepper powders, sugar and salt. Heat 2 tablespoon mustard oil. Temper with the dry red chillies and bay leaves. When they change their colour, add the banana flower mixture. Stir fry for a minute. Add the fried dal balls; stir. Cover and cook over medium heat till the water almost evaporates and the whole thing looks wet. Remove and garnish with grated coconut. Serve at room temperature with rice.

The cutting of mocha or banana flower is a delicate art. Before you proceed, grease your palms with a little mustard oil. Remove the large outer petals and take out the white flowers from the base. You will find a transparent petal at the end of each flower and a white matchlike stick inside. Discard these from each flower individually. Now, take a bunch of flowers and cut into small pieces. Put these in a bowl containing water and soak for, at least 15 minutes.

Rogan Josh of Cabbage

Ingredients (Serves 6)

- 1 tbsp ghee
- 10 peppercorns
- 5 cloves
- 2.5 cm stick of cinnamon
- 2 black cardamoms
- 5 red chillies
- 1 tbsp aniseeds
- 1/2 tsp dry ginger powder
- 4 small cabbages
- 2 cups thick curd
- Salt to taste
- 1 tbsp mustard oil
- A pinch of asafoetida
- 1 tbsp shahjeera

Preparation

Heat 1 teaspoon ghee in a frying pan and roast the peppercorns, cinnamon, black cardamoms (seeds only), red chillies, and aniseeds lightly. Grind to a powder and add the ginger powder. Wash the whole cabbages, discarding any wilted or discoloured outer leaves. Cut into 2 cm rings. Marinate in whipped curd for half an hour. Heat the mustard oil till it smokes. Remove from heat; let it cool a little. Put on heat again and add the ghee. Temper with asafoetida and shahjeera. Add the cabbage and fry for 5 minutes over high heat. Add salt to taste and 1/2 cup of water. Cover and cook till crisp and tender. Sprinkle the powdered spices over the cabbage. Mix well and cook. Keep stirring till the moisture evaporates. Serve hot with chappatis.

Aloo Khosha Bhaja (Fried Potato Peels)

Ingredients (Serves 4)

- Peel of 2 medium potatoes
- 1/4 cup flour
- 1 tbsp rice flour
- 1/2 tbsp poppy seeds
- A pinch of soda bicarb
- 1/4 tsp kalonji
- Salt and chilli powder to taste
- Mustard oil for deep frying

Preparation

Peel the potatoes a little thick. Finely shred the peels. Mix the flour, rice flour, soda and the remaining ingredients together. Add enough water and the peels to make a batter of pakoda consistency. Add 2 teaspoon hot oil. Heat enough oil in a karahi for deep frying. Drop spoonfuls of the batter in hot oil till a golden brown. Drain and keep aside. Serve hot with tomato ketchup.

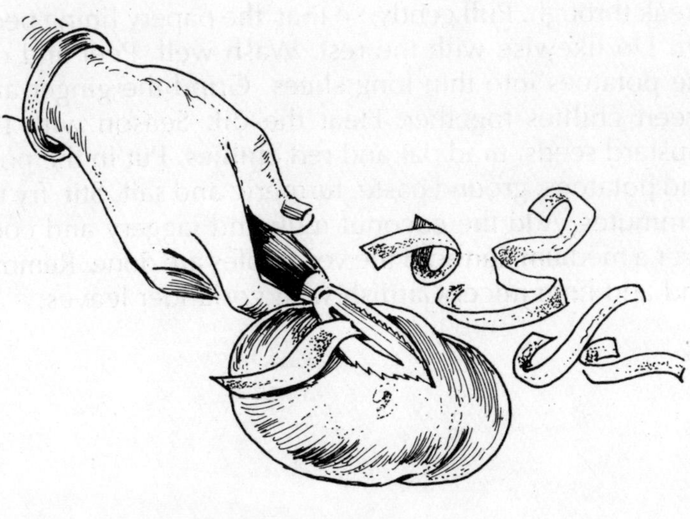

Spicy Pea Pods

Ingredients (Serves 4)

- Pods of 250 gm fresh tender peas
- 2 medium potatoes
- 2 cm piece of ginger
- 2 green chillies
- 2 tbsp refined oil
- 1 tsp mustard seeds
- 1 tsp urad dal
- 2 dry red chillies
- 1/2 tsp turmeric powder
- Salt to taste
- 1 cup thick coconut milk
- Grated jaggery or sugar to taste
- 1 tbsp lime juice
- 1/3 cup chopped fresh coriander leaves

Preparation

The pea pods should be fresh and free from blemishes. Divide each pod into two. Holding each part, stalk upwards, with the inner part facing you, bend the stalk end inwards about 1 cm down till it cracks but does not break through. Pull gently, so that the papery lining peels off. Do likewise with the rest. Wash well. Peel and cut the potatoes into thin long slices. Grind the ginger and green chillies together. Heat the oil. Season with the mustard seeds, urad dal and red chillies. Put in the pods and potatoes, ground paste, turmeric and salt. Stir fry for 5 minutes. Add the coconut milk and jaggery and cook over a medium flame till the vegetables are done. Remove and add lime juice. Garnish with coriander leaves.

Nutty Knol Khol

Ingredients (Serves 4)

- 4 large knol khols (ganth gobi)
- 2 large onions
- $2^1/_2$ tbsp refined oil
- 2 bay leaves
- 20 cashewnuts
- Salt to taste
- 1/2 tbsp ghee
- 25 raisins
- 1 tsp sugar

Grind together

- 2 cm piece of ginger
- 10 cloves of garlic
- 2 tbsp fresh coriander leaves
- 2 green chillies
- 1 tbsp poppy seeds
- 1 tsp coriander seeds
- 1/2 tsp cumin seeds
- 1/2 tsp chilli powder
- 1/2 tsp turmeric powder

Roast and Powder

- 4 cloves
- 2 green cardamoms
- 2.5 cm stick of cinnamon
- 5 peppercorns
- A piece of mace
- 1/4 nutmeg

Preparation

Peel and cut the knol khol into small cubes. Thinly slice the onion. Heat the oil in a karahi. Temper with the bay leaves. When it turns a shade darker, add the onions. Fry till a light brown. Add the ground paste alongwith a tablespoon of water. Fry over a medium heat, stirring well till light brown and the oil leaves the spices. Add the cashewnuts, knol khol, salt and 2 cups of water. Stir to mix well. Cover when it comes to a boil. Simmer till the knol khols are done. Heat the ghee in a small frying pan. Add the raisins. They will puff up at once. Add to the gravy alongwith the sugar and roasted and powdered masala. Cook for 5 minutes and remove. The gravy should be thick.

Variation : A lot of other vegetables can be cooked the same way like turnips, papaya, potatoes, or a combination of vegetables.

Rajasthani Panchmeli
Mixed Vegetable Curry from Rajasthan

Ingredients (Serves 4)

- 100 gm tinda
- 100 gm cucumber
- 100 gm cluster beans (guar phali)
- 25 gm magodi (moong dal vadis)
- 1 tsp salt
- 1/2 tsp turmeric powder
- 2 tsp chilli powder
- 2 tsp amchur powder
- 3 tbsp refined oil
- A pinch of asafoetida
- 1 tsp cumin seeds
- 2 tsp sugar

Preparation

Peel tinda and cucumber. Cut all vegetables into 2.5 cm long sticks. Parboil the cluster beans, tinda and mangodi. Strain, but reserve the stock. Mix salt, turmeric, chilli and amchur powders with the vegetables and keep aside. Heat the oil in a karahi and temper with the asafoetida and cumin seeds. Add the parboiled vegetables, mangodi and cucumber and stir fry for 5 minutes, along with a tablespoon of water. When the oil floats on top, add the sugar. Mix and serve hot with chappatis.

Variation: In Rajasthan, kachri is used as the souring agent. Since kachri is not easily available outside Rajasthan, I've taken the liberty to substitute amchur. But do use kachri, if you can get it.

Sabz Khada Masala

Punjabi Malai Palak

Gobhi Mussalam

Alu ki Sabzi

Cauliflower Supreme

Baghare Baigan

MIX&MATCH

Bhindani Kadhi (Ladies Finger in Curd)

Ingredients (Serves 8)

- 125 gm small tender bhindis
- 2 tbsp coriander powder
- 1 tsp chilli powder
- 1/2 tsp amchur powder
- 1 tsp salt
- 1/4 tsp turmeric powder
- 6 tbsp gramflour
- 1 tsp ghee
- Oil for frying

Kadhi

- 225 gm curd
- 3 tbsp gramflour
- 1 tbsp refined oil
- 3/4 tsp cumin seeds
- 3/4 tsp mustard seeds
- A pinch of asafoetida
- 1/4 tsp chilli powder
- 3/4 tsp turmeric powder
- 3/4 tsp grated ginger
- 2 green chillies, chopped
- Salt to taste

Preparation

Wash and pat dry the bhindis. Cut off the tops and slit leng thwise, but do not cut through. Mix all the ingredients except the gramflour, oil and 1/4 teaspoon salt. Stuff the bhindis with the spices. Prepare a batter of pakoda consistency with the gram flour, salt and water. Add 1 tablespoon hot oil. Heat enough oil for deep frying in a karahi. Dip the bhindis in the batter and fry to a golden brown.

Kadhi: Beat the curd with the gramflour and 3 cups of water till smooth. Add another 3 cups of water. Heat the oil. Add the cumin, mustard seeds and asafoetida. When they stop sizzling, add chilli, turmeric and the gramflour-curd mixture. Stir constantly till it comes to a boil. Add ginger, green chillies and salt. Let it cook on a slow fire for half an hour. Heat the kadhi and add the fried bhindi at the time of serving.

Variation: Any other vegetable can be fried this way and added to the kadhi.

Stuffed Dal Dhokli

Ingredients (Serves 6)

- 100 gm shelled peas
- 4 green chillies
- 2 cm piece of ginger
- 250 gm arhar dal
- 2 tsp salt
- 1/4 tsp turmeric powder
- 1/2 tsp coriander powder
- 1/2 tsp cumin powder
- 50 gm jaggery
- 2 tbsp shelled peanuts
- 1 tbsp refined oil
- 2 whole dry chillies
- 1 tsp mustard seeds
- 1 sprig curry leaves
- 1/4 tsp sesame seeds
- A pinch of asafoetida
- 1 tsp chilli powder
- 4 tbsp grated coconut
- 2 tbsp chopped fresh coriander
- 1 tbsp sugar
- 1 tsp lime juice
- 1 tbsp ghee
- 225 gm atta
- Refined oil for frying

Preparation

Boil the peas and mash well. Grind the green chillies and ginger together. Boil the dal in 2 litres of water. Add 1/2 teaspoon salt, turmeric, coriander, cumin, jaggery and peanuts. Let it cook over medium heat till the dal is well done. Heat the oil in a small saucepan. Add the whole dry chillies and mustard seeds. When the chillies turn dark, add the curry leaves, sesame seeds and asafoetida. Remove from heat; add the chilli powder and pour over the dal. When everything gets well mixed, the dal should get totally mashed. Keep aside. Mix the grated coconut, fresh coriander, mashed peas, green chilli-ginger paste, 1/2 teaspoon salt, sugar and lime juice together. Divide into 25 portions. Rub the ghee well into the atta. Knead to form a soft dough with water. Divide into 25 small balls. Roll into thin puris with the help of a little dry atta. Place one portion of the filling on one side of the puri and cover with the other. This will give it a half moon shape. Press the edges well. Heat enough oil in a karahi and deep fry the dhoklis till a light golden brown. Heat the dal before serving. Add the fried dhoklis and boil for 5 minutes. Serve hot.

Variation: Instead of frying the dhoklis, they may be added to the dal raw and cooked along with the seasoning.

Avial

Vegetable Curry from Kerala

Ingredients (Serves 6)

- 100 gm drumsticks
- 100 gm yam
- 1 large raw banana
- 100 gm ash gourd
- 100 gm long beans
- 1 large coconut
- 2 green chillies
- 1 tsp cuminseeds
- 5-6 curry leaves
- Salt to taste
- 1/2 tsp turmeric powder
- 1 tsp chilli powder
- 1 tbsp refined oil

Preparation

Peel and cut the vegetables into 2.5 cm long pieces. Grate the coconut and grind along with the green chillies, cuminseeds and curry leaves. Cook the vegetables with 2 cups of water, salt, turmeric and chilli powder till tender. But do not overcook. The vegetables should not lose their shape. Add the ground paste and oil. Mix well. Simmer for 5 minutes and remove.

Variation: Keralites use coconut oil. Feel free to use it, if you want. Other vegetables like bottle gourd, ridge gourd, snake gourd, potato, carrot, beans etc. may also be used. Sometimes a little curd is added, too.

Khatta Meetha Karela (Sweet Sour Bitter Gourd)

Ingredients (Serves 6)

- 3 large bitter gourds
- Salt to taste
- 3/4 tsp turmeric powder
- 1 tbsp thick tamarind paste
- 1 lime-sized ball of jaggery
- 2 tbsp mustard oil
- 1 tsp paanch phoran
- A pinch of asafoetida
- 1$^{1}/_{2}$ tsp chilli powder
- 2 tsp coriander powder
- 1/2 tsp amchur powder

Preparation

Lightly scrape the bitter gourd and cut into 1/2 inch rings. Smear with 1 teaspoon salt and 1/2 teaspoon turmeric; leave aside for half an hour. Squeeze and wash well. Boil in lightly salted water till crisp tender. Strain and press the karelas to get rid of the moisture. Boil the tamarind paste and jaggery in 1/2 cup of water till the jaggery dissolves. Strain. Heat the oil in a karahi; season with the 'paanch phoran' and asafoetida. When they splutter, add the bitter gourd and fry over a medium heat till golden brown; about 4-5 minutes. Add 1 teaspoon salt, 1/2 teaspoon turmeric, chilli, coriander and amchur powders and stir for another 3-4 minutes over a low heat. If needed, sprinkle a tablespoon of water. Now, keep adding a little tamarind water at a time till all of it is used up. Keep stirring during the process. The gravy should have a thick consistency. Serve hot. Goes well with stuffed parathas.

Tenga

Assamese Vegetable Curry

Ingredients (Serves 4)

- 2 large ridge gourd
- 4 parwals
- 100 gm bottle gourd
- 100 gm ash gourd
- 1 squash
- 150 gm paneer
- 4 green chillies
- 1 tbsp mustard oil
- 1/2 tsp fenugreek seeds
- 1 tsp turmeric powder
- Salt to taste
- $1^1/_2$ tbsp lime juice

Preparation

Peel the ridge gourd and slice into 2.5 cm roundels. Peel the parwal at regular intervals and slice likewise into circles. Peel and slice the bottle gourd and squash into thin pieces. Dice the paneer. Slit the green chillies. Heat the oil in a karahi till it smokes; temper with the fenugreek seeds. When they turn a shade darker, add all the vegetables. Stir fry for 3-4 minutes on high heat. Mix the turmeric with 1 tablespoon water and add to the vegetables. Stir fry for another minute. Add $1^1/_2$ cups of water, salt and green chillies. Cover and cook over medium heat. When the vegetables are half done, add the paneer, Add the lime juice when the vegetables are cooked. Remove from fire. This has a soupy gravy. Looks a light golden brown and tastes pleasantly tart.

Variation: Use all or any of the vegetables listed above. Tamarind or tomato can replace lime juice as the souring agent. Any small fish like puti or mourala can be lightly fried and added in the end.

Baked Pumpkin

You have no idea how delicious a mundane vegetable like the pumpkin can be unless you've tasted the following recipe. Baked this way, the pumpkin can give the roasted steak a run for its money.

Ingredients (Serves 4)

- 1 kg pumpkin
- 2 tbsp butter
- Salt and freshly ground pepper to taste

Preparation

Remove the seeds of the pumpkin. Wash and pat dry. Cut into fairly large pieces but do not peel. Take a flat baking tin and grease with a little oil. Brush the pumpkin with the butter and lay on the baking tin. Do not overlap. Sprinkle with salt and a generous quantity of freshly ground pepper. Roast in oven preheated to 380°F/190°C till done, turning the pumpkin a few times.

Sookha Arbi (Dry Colocasia Curry)

Ingredients (Serves 4-6)

- 250 gm arbi
- 2 tbsp refined oil or ghee
- 1/2 tsp garam masala powder
- 1 tbsp amchur powder
- 1 tsp ajwain
- Salt to taste

Roast and powder coarsely

- 1 tbsp coriander seeds
- 1 tbsp cumin seeds
- 4-6 dry red chillies
- A pinch of fenugreek seeds

Preparation

Wash and boil the arbi till just done. Do not overcook. Peel and cut each into two. Heat the oil or ghee in a skillet. Place the arbi halves in a layer over medium high flame. Add half the roasted spices. The spices should get well coated over the arbi pieces. When the underside is golden, turn over and sprinkle with the remaining roasted spices, garam masala, amchur, ajwain and salt. When the arbis are golden brown from both sides and the spices well coated over it, remove from fire. Serve with chappatis or parathas.

Baked Vegetables in Orange Sauce

Ingredients (Serves 2)

- 250 gm pumpkin
- 1 sweet potato
- 1 large carrot
- Salt to taste
- 2 green chillies
- A pinch of saffron
- 1/4 cup of milk
- 1 tbsp grated orange peel
- A pinch of cardamom powder

For Sauce

- 100 ml fresh orange juice
- 1 tsp sugar
- 1 tsp butter
- 1 tsp cornflour
- 1/4 tsp white pepper powder

Preparation

Sauce: Heat the butter. Put the orange juice, sugar and boil. When reduced by half, add the cornflour. Boil till it thickens a little. Sprinkle white pepper.

Peel and cut the pumpkin in flat pieces. Parboil, peel and slice sweet potato and carrot into roundels. Chop the green chillies. Grease a baking dish. Place the vegetables in layers. Sprinkle salt and green chillies in between the layers. Mix the saffron, milk, grated orange peel and cardamom powder. Sprinkle all over the vegetables. Cover with a foil. Bake in a 350°F/180°C oven for 35-40 minutes, uncovering for the last 15 minutes or till the vegetables are tender. Remove. Pour sauce all over and serve.

THAI RED CURRY

Ingredients (Serves 4)

- 2 coconuts
- 8 button mushrooms
- 1 medium carrot
- 150 gm paneer
- 4 large cauliflower florets
- 5 babycorns
- 10-12 basil leaves
- 1 stalk lemon grass
- 8 cloves garlic
- 12 Kashmiri chillies
- 3 tbsp refined oil
- 1/2 cup shelled green peas
  Juice of 1 lime
- A dash of soya sauce
- 2 tbsp brown sugar
- Salt to taste

Preparation

Grate the coconut. Take out the first extraction of coconut milk using 1 cup of hot water; then take out the second extraction using 2 cups of hot water; then take out the second extraction using 2 cups of hot water. Keep the two separate. Dice the mushrooms, carrot, cauliflower florets and paneer into small cubes. Slice the babycorns, chop the basil leaves and lemon grass—white part only. Grind the Kashmiri chillies and garlic together. Heat the oil in a karahi; add the ground paste and stir fry. Add the second extraction of the coconut milk. Stir constantly till the mixture starts to boil. Add the vegetables and the remaining ingredients. Boil on medium heat till the vegetables are done. Stir the first extraction of the coconut milk and remove from fire. There should be some gravy. Serve with fried rice.

Variation: Non-vegetarians may use nam-pla (Thai fish sauce) in place of soya sauce. In case you want a thick gravy, mix 1 tablespoon cornflour.

For white curry: Use only garlic-green chilli paste. Omit Kashmiri chillies.

For green curry: Omit Kashmiri chilli. Use green chilli and 1 cup of coriander leaves ground together.

PRESSED RICE AND POTATO CURRY

Ingredients (Serves 2)

- 100 gm pressed rice
- Mustard oil as needed
- 1 large potato
- 1/2 coconut, sliced
- 1 tbsp ghee
- 2 green cardamoms
- 4 sticks cinnamon
- 15 raisins
- 1/4 cup onion paste
- 1/2 tsp turmeric powder
- 1 tsp cumin powder
- 1 tsp chilli powder
- Salt to taste
- 1/2 tsp sugar
- 4 green chillies, slit
- 1/2 tsp garam masala powder

Preparation

Fry the pressed rice in hot mustard oil. It takes only a few seconds. Remove with a perforated spoon onto a piece of paper so that extra oil can drain out. Peel and dice the potatoes and coconut slices. Heat 1 tablespoon mustard oil in a karahi. Let it smoke, then add the ghee. Add coarsely powdered green cardamom and cinnamon. When these turn a shade darker, add the raisins. These will puff up at once. Add the onion paste and saute till pink. Add potatoes and coconut and stir fry for 2 minutes. Add the turmeric, cumin and chilli powders one after the other, stirring after each addition. Sprinkle a little water if necessary. Add the salt, sugar and slit green chillies. Stir and add the fried pressed rice and 1 cup of water. Cover and cook for 5 minutes. Mix with a ladle so that the potatoes and pressed rice get mashed and mixed. Sprinkle the garam masala powder and remove.

Variation: Cauliflower and peas may be included. If using cauliflower, fry lightly before cooking.

Fried fish head can also be added.

Sabji Makhani
(Vegetables in Butter)

Ingredients (Serves 6)

- 100 gm carrots
- 150 gm cauliflower
- I cup shelled peas
- 100 gm French beans
- 2 cm ginger
- 4 cloves garlic
- 150 ml curd
- 2 tsp Kashmiri chilli powder
- 1/2 tsp garam masala powder
- Juice of 1 lime
- 100 gm butter
- 2 tbsp tomato ketchup
- 2 tbsp finely chopped fresh coriander leaves
- 1/2 cup cream

Preparation

Wash and cut all the vegetables into small cubes. Parboil in water. Reserve the stock. Grind the ginger and garlic. Beat the curd and add the ground ginger-garlic, Kashmiri chilli powder, 1/4 teaspoon garam masala powder and lime juice. Mix well. Heat the ghee in a karahi, add the curd mixture and stir fry evenly till the ghee separates. Stir in 1 cup of the reserved vegetable stock and parboiled vegetables; stir over a high heat. Lower heat when the gravy thickens. Add ketchup, coriander leaves and remove from fire.

Put in the cream and remaining garam masala. Mix and serve. Garnish with finely chopped coriander leaves.

Potato Dum Pukht

Ingredients (Serves 6)

- 10-12 potatoes, approximately 500 gm
- 2 tbsp grated khoya
- 2 medium onions
- 100 gm ghee
- 10 almonds, blanched
- 25 raisins
- 4 green cardamoms
- 5 cloves
- 5 cm piece of cinnamon
- 1 pinch of saffron, soaked in warm milk
- 1/2 tsp ginger paste
- 1 tbsp Kashmiri chilli powder
- Salt to taste
- 1 tsp sugar

Preparation

Peel the potatoes. Soak in water till it is used. Slice an onion thinly and evenly. Fry in ghee till brown. Remove on a piece of paper so that the extra ghee can drain out. Grind the other onion. Grind together the blanched almonds, raisins, cloves, green cardamom and cinnamon to a smooth paste. Mix the saffron. Heat the ghee left from frying the onions and fry the potatoes till a light brown. Remove. Beat the curd and mix the ground onion, ginger paste, ground paste, chilli powder, salt and sugar. Take a degchi or preferably a handi. Heat the ghee; add the curd mixture and fried potatoes. Mix well. Seal the pan with atta dough and put on dum with a tawa underneath for half an hour. Break seal before serving. Garnish with the fried onion and grated khoya. This should have no gravy save what is clinging to the potatoes. Serve with pulao, naans or parathas.

Variation : Cauliflower cooked this way is just as good.

Dilpasand Kofta (Jackfruit Kofta Curry)

Ingredients (Serves 6)

For Koftas

- 1/2 kg raw jackfruit
- 1 medium potato
- 2 tbsp refined oil
- 2 bread slices
- 2 tbsp atta
- 1/2 tsp chilli powder
- 1 pinch turmeric powder
- 1 tsp coriander powder
- 1/2 tsp garam masala powder
- 1 tbsp chopped fresh coriander leaves
- 100 gm khoya, grated
- 1 tsp salt
- Refined oil for frying the koftas

For Gravy

- 50 gm ghee
- A pinch of asafoetida
- 100 gm curd
- 1/2 tsp turmeric powder
- 1/2 tsp sugar
- 1/2 tsp chilli powder
- 1 tsp coriander powder
- 1 tsp ginger paste
- Salt to taste
- 1 tsp garam masala powder
- A pinch of saffron
- 1 tbsp kewra water

Preparation

Kofta : Peel and cut jackfruit into cubes. Boil jackfruits and potatoes till just done. Do not overcook. Mash jackfruits and potato separately. Heat the oil in a karahi. Add the mashed jackfruit and all the ingredients except bread slices, atta and potato. Stir fry till the moisture evaporates. When cool enough to handle, add the mashed potatoes and the bread slices, soaked in water and squeezed dry. Mix well to make a dough. Make lemon-sized balls. Roll in atta and deep fry in oil till golden,keep aside.

Gravy : Heat the ghee in a karahi. Add asafoetida. Beat the curd and add all the spices except garam masala and saffron. Stir fry over medium heat till the oil surfaces.

Add $1^1/_2$ cups of water and the koftas. Cook for 10 minutes. Add the saffron mixed with 1 tablespoon kewra water and garam masala powder. Garnish with chopped almonds (optional).

Cauliflower Supreme

Ingredients (Serves 4)

- 2 medium cauliflowers
- 1 tbsp butter
- 1 tbsp chopped parsley
- 1/2 tsp paprika or Kashmiri chilli powder
- 3 slices of bread
- Refined oil for frying and breads
- 1/4 cup grated cheese

For cheese sauce

- 2 tbsp butter
- 2 tbsp flour
- 2 cups milk
- 1/4 tsp salt
- 1/4 tsp pepper powder
- 1/2 cup grated cheese
- 1/4 cup cream
- 1/4 cup cream
- 1/4 tsp chilli powder

Preparation

Cut the cauliflower into florets. Boil in salted water for 2 minutes. Drain. Wash in cold water. Keep aside. Heat the butter. Add the chopped parsley and blanched cauliflorets, sprinkle with the paprika. Toss for 2 minutes. Set aside. Discard the sides and cut the bread slices into 4 triangles each. Deep fry in hot oil and drain onto paper towels.

Cheese sauce: Melt the butter in a saucepan and add the flour. Stir till the flour is cooked; add milk. Cook, stirring constantly till the sauce boils. Remove from the heat. Add the salt, pepper and cheese. Mix well. Mix the cauliflorets with the cheese sauce. Place in 16 cm baking dish. Sprinkle 1/4 cup grated cheese on top. Pour the cream mixture on top in streaks. Place in a oven preheated to 375° F/180° C for 20 minutes. Place the deep fried breads on the side of the dish and serve.

Variation : Use tender corn and mushroom the same way. A whole cauliflower may be boiled and baked the same way.

Yam and Pea Keema

Ingredients (Serves 4)

- 250 gm yam
- 2 large onions
- 2 tomatoes
- 100 ml refined oil
- 2 bay leaves
- 1/2 tsp garlic paste
- 1 tsp ginger paste
- 1 tsp chilli powder
- 2 tsp coriander powder
- 1 cup shelled peas
- Salt to taste
- 1 tsp garam masala powder
- Coriander leaves for garnishing

Preparation

Peel and cut yam into small cubes. Boil till tender. Grind onions. Finely chop tomatoes. Heat half the oil in a karahi. Fry the yam pieces till light brown. Remove. Add the remaining oil to the oil in the karahi. Add the bay leaves. When it changes colour, add the onion paste and fry till light brown. Add the garlic paste and fry till the raw smell of the garlic disappears. Put in the ginger paste, chilli and coriander powders and tomatoes and fry over a low heat till the oil separates. Add the yam and peas and stir for 2 minutes. Add $1^1/_2$ cups of water and salt. Cover and cook over a low heat. Keep stirring often. When everything gets mixed, add the garam masala powder and remove. The yam may disintegrate. Never mind, this is how it should be. Garnish with coriander leaves. Goes well with rotis, parathas and naans.

Navratan Korma (Exotic Vegetable Curry)

Ingredients (Serves 6)

- 1 medium cauliflower
- 8 French beans
- 1 large carrot
- 1 medium potato
- 1 cup shelled peas
- 1 large capsicum
- 15 almonds
- 20 sultanas (munakka)
- 1 large coconut
- 1 cup milk
- 2.5 cm ginger
- 2 tbsp poppy seeds
- 1/3 cup ghee
- 2 bay leaves
- 4 cloves
- 4 green cardamoms
- 5 cm stick of cinnamon
- 1 tsp sugar
- 20 cashewnuts
- 100 gm paneer, diced
- Salt to taste
- 1/2 cup cream
- 1 tsp garam masala powder
- Juice of 1 lime
- A handful of chopped fresh coriander leaves

Preparation

Parboil all the vegetables except capsicum. Cut cauliflower into small florets, potato and carrot into medium cubes and French beans into 4 pieces. Halve the capsicum; deseed and cut into square pieces. Blanch the almonds and deskin. Soak sultanas in hot water for half an hour. Grate the coconut. Add 1 tablespoon hot water and extract the thick coconut milk. Heat milk; add to the coconut, blend and extract the second lot of thin coconut milk. Keep the two extractions separate. Grind the ginger and poppy seeds. Heat the ghee in a karahi. Add the bay leaves, cloves, cardamoms and cinnamon. When they change colour, add the ginger paste. Fry for 30 seconds. Add the vegetables and stir fry for 2 minutes. Add the ginger-poppy seed paste, second extraction of coconut milk, sugar, salt, pepper, almonds, munakka, cashewnuts and paneer. Keep stirring well. Cover and cook over medium heat till the vegetables are done. Add the thick coconut milk, cream and garam masala powder. Cook for 5 minutes. Do not let it boil. Remove and stir in the lime juice. Garnish with chopped fresh coriander.

Variation: Use 1 red and 1 green capsicum, broccoli, baby corn, mushroom. If you add Kashmiri chilli powder and beetroot, the curry will take a lovely pink colour. Instead of dry fruits, chopped fresh fruits like apples, pear, pineapple, grapes can be used. Add just before removing from fire along with 2 tablespoon of grated khoya.

Gobhi Musallam (Whole Cauliflower Baked)

Ingredients (Serves 4)

- 1 medium cauliflower
- 2.5 cm piece of ginger
- 6 cloves garlic
- 2 green chillies
- 1/2 tsp salt
- 1/2 tsp chilli powder
- 1/2 tsp garam masala powder
- 2 tsp lime juice

For Masala

- 2 large onions
- 5 cloves of garlic
- 3 medium tomatoes
- 2.5 cm piece of ginger
- 1 tsp coriander seeds
- 1/2 tsp cumin seeds
- 6 cloves
- 8 peppercorns
- 2 green cardamoms
- A pinch of nutmeg
- 2.5 cm stick of cinnamon
- 2 tbsp refined oil
- 4 tbsp curd
- 3/4 tsp salt
- 1/2 tsp garam masala powder
- A handful of chopped fresh coriander leaves

Preparation

Keep the cauliflower whole. Cut off the stem as close to the flower as possible. Give a crosswise cut on the base of the cauliflower. Wash and dry. Grind the ginger, garlic and green chillies together. Add the salt, chilli powder, garam masala powder and lime juice with the ground paste. Insert the paste between the florets. Place the cauliflower, stem downwards, into a bowl. Transfer this to a trivet in the pressure cooker. Add 3/4 glass of water and steam for 2 minutes only, after the cooker reaches full pressure. Take out the cauliflower and keep aside.

Masala : Thinly slice the onion and garlic. Blanch and chop the tomatoes. Grind the coriander seeds, cumin, cloves, peppercorns, cinnamon, cardamom and nutmeg together.

Heat the oil and fry onion and garlic till soft. Add the ground spices and continue cooking; stir well. Add a little curd at a time and stir until it is completely utilised. Lastly add the tomatoes. Cook till the tomatoes are well mixed and oil floats on top. Lightly grease a baking dish. Put the cauliflower in it and cover with the masala and bake in an oven preheated to 350° F / 180° C for 15 minutes. Sprinkle garam masala powder and chopped fresh coriander. Serve hot.

Variation: You may add some minced mutton or chicken in the masala and stuff the cauliflower with it.

Shahi Stuffed Tomatoes

Ingredients (Serves 4)

- 8 medium tomatoes
- A generous pinch each of salt pepper and chilli powder
- 1 tsp sugar

For Filling

- 1/2 cup shelled peas
- 1 small onion
- 2 green chillies
- 50 gm paneer
- 2 tbsp cashewnuts
- 1 tbsp ghee (do not use oil)
- 3 tbsp cream
- Salt to taste
- 1/2 tsp pepper

For Gravy

- 2 large onions
- 6 cloves garlic
- 3 tbsp ghee
- 1 tsp chilli powder
- 1 tbsp coriander powder
- 1/2 tsp cumin powder.
- 2.5 cm ginger
- 1 tsp garam masala powder
- 2 tbsp chopped green coriander leaves

Preparation

Cut a slice from the stem end of each tomato. Take out the seeds and pith and reserve. Mix the salt, pepper, chilli powder and sugar. Sprinkle a little of the mixture in each of the tomatoes. Invert and keep aside for 20 minutes.

Filling: Boil the peas. Finely chop the onion and green chillies. Cut the paneer and cashewnuts into small pieces. Heat the ghee and saute the onion till pink. Add the cashew and fry for a couple of minutes. Add the peas and stir for a minute. Add paneer and fry for 1 minute. Stir in the cream and cook for 5 minutes on low heat. Finally add salt, pepper and green chillies. Mix well; check seasoning. Remove. Fill the tomatoes with this mixture. Bake in an oven preheated to 190°C/375°F for 15-20 minutes.

Gravy: Strain the removed parts of the tomatoes to obtain a puree. Grind onion and garlic together. Grind the ginger separately. Heat the ghee in a karahi and fry the ground paste till golden brown. Add the chilli powder and stir for one minute. Add 1 tablespoon water. Add coriander and cumin powders and ground ginger. Fry for 5 minutes on low heat. Add the tomato puree and salt and cook. Stirring, till the ghee separates. Add 1 glass of water and simmer for 10 minutes. Remove from fire and add the garam masala. Pour the gravy on a shallow dish, arrange the tomatoes on it, garnish with coriander leaves.

Variation: Use cooked prawns, boiled fish or cooked mince for a non-vegetarian filling in place of paneer.

Garden Surprise

Ingredients (Serves 6)

- 100 gm French beans
- 100 gm carrots
- 1 large capsicum
- 200 g small potatoes
- 100 gm small onions
- 1/2 cup shelled green peas
- 250 gm tomatoes
- 2 tbsp refined oil
- 2 tbsp ghee
- 1/4 cup cream
- Salt and sugar to taste
- Coriander leaves for garnishing

Grind to a paste

- 1 onion
- 3 cloves of garlic
- 2 fresh red chillies
- 1/4 cup grated coconut
- 1 tbsp magaj
- 2 tbsp vinegar

Roast and powder

- 3 green cardamoms
- 2.5 cm piece of cinnamon
- 2 cloves

Preparation

Cut the beans and carrots into long strips. Chop the capsicum in small square pieces. Peel and boil the potatoes and onions, keeping them whole. Parboil the beans, carrots and peas together. Heat oil in a karahi and deep fry the potatoes and remove. Blend the tomatoes in the mixie and strain the puree. Heat the oil and ghee together in a karahi. Fry the paste on a medium heat till the ghee separates. Add the capsicum and fry, while stirring continually. Add the vegetables, tomato puree, salt and sugar. Cover and cook for 5 minutes. Lastly, add the cream and powdered masala. Sprinkle coriander leaves and serve hot.

Sabz Kabab Kalia

Ingredients (Serves 6)

For Kabab

- 1/2 kg potatoes
- 2 tbsp flour
- Salt to taste
- Refined oil for frying

For Filling

- 1 cup mixed vegetables
- 6 cashewnuts
- 10 raisins
- Pinch of salt
- 1 tbsp refined oil
- 1 tbsp fresh coriander leaves
- 2-3 green chillies
- 1/2 tsp garam masala powder

Grind together

- 2 tbsp grated coconut
- 1 small onion
- 4 cloves of garlic
- 1 cm piece of ginger
- 2 tsp poppy seeds
- 1 tbsp coriander seeds
- 1 tsp cumin seeds
- 2.5 cm cinnamon
- 2 cloves
- 2 green cardamoms

For Gravy

- 3 tbsp refined oil
- 1 tbsp ghee
- 1/2 tsp turmeric powder
- 1/2 tsp chilli powder
- 1/2 cup cream
- 1/2 cup curd
- Salt to taste
- 1/2 tsp sugar

Preparation

Filling: Mixed vegetables, include peas, carrots, beans and cauliflower. Cut them into small pieces and boil. Chop the cashewnuts, raisins and green chillies. Heat the oil in a karahi. Add the vegetables along with the rest of the ingredients. Mix well and cool. The filling should remain soft and not over fried.

Kabab: Boil, peel and mash the potatoes, till smooth. Mix flour and salt. Divide into 12 portions. Place one portion of filling inside and shape into kababs. Shallow fry in a skillet till golden, using refined oil. Keep hot.

Gravy: Heat the oil and ghee together in a karahi. Add the ground paste and turmeric and chilli powders.

Fry over medium heat, stirring till the oil separates. Add 2 cups of water. Cover and cook over a medium heat for 10 minutes. Remove. Let it cool a little. Now, blend in the mixie and strain. Pour the strained gravy in the same karahi and put on a medium heat. Add the cream, beaten curd, salt and sugar. Add a little water, if you find it too thick. Lower the heat once the gravy comes to a boil and cook, while stirring continually till medium thick. Place the cutlets in a deep plate and pour the hot gravy over. Garnish with silver foil and tomato rings.

Variation: The kababs can be served by themselves as snacks. In that case, coat with breadcrumbs and deep fry.

Saag ko Jharekho (Nepalese Stir Fried Greens)

Ingredients (Serves 4)

- 1 large bunch spinach
- 1 large bunch fresh fenugreek leaves
- 1 chinese cabbage
- 2 tsp ghee
- 1/2 tsp fenugreek seeds
- 1/2 tsp kalonji
- 2 whole red chillies
- 1 tsp ginger paste
- Salt to taste
- 1/2 tsp sugar
- 1/2 tsp chaat masala

Preparation

Wash well and finely chop the greens. Heat the ghee in a karahi. Add the fenugreek seeds, kalonji and the chillies, broken into two. Add the greens and stir fry. Once they release their water, add the ginger paste, salt and sugar. Cook on high heat, uncovered, stirring continually. Remove when the moisture evaporates completely. Sprinkle the chaat masala and serve with hot boiled rice.

Variation: If unable to obtain chinese cabbage use the tender parts of ordinary cabbage.

VEGETABLE JHAL FREZIE

Ingredients (Serves 4)

- 1 medium potato
- 1 small carrot
- 5 beans
- 1/2 cup shelled peas
- 1 medium capsicum
- 1/2 cup cabbage
- 5 medium cauliflorets
- 2 medium tomatoes
- 1/2 cup cream or top layer of the milk
- Salt and pepper to taste
- 1/2 tsp garam masala powder
- 2 tbsp ghee or butter

Preparation

Peel the potatoes and carrots. Cut into long strips. String and cut beans into 2-3 pieces each. Deseed and cut the capsicum into square pieces. Shred the cabbage. Chop the tomatoes. Parboil potatoes, carrots, beans, peas and cauliflorets. Do not overcook. Strain. Heat the ghee, saute the capsicum for one minute, then add the cabbage and tomatoes. Saute after each addition. Add the boiled vegetables, salt, pepper, garam masala and cream. Cover and cook on a slow fire for 5-7 minutes, stirring a few times in between. The gravy should be thick.

Sarson ka Saag (Curried Mustard Greens)

Ingredients (Serves 6)

- 500 gm mustard greens, preferably with flowers
- 200 gm spinach leaves
- 50 gm bathua greens (optional)
- 2 green chillies
- 2 cm piece of ginger
- 1/2 tsp turmeric powder
- 1 tsp powdered jaggery
- 2-3 tbsp cornmeal (makki ki atta)
- 2 tbsp butter or ghee
- 1 large onion, finely chopped
- A small piece of ginger, grated
- 1/4 tsp red chilli powder

Preparation

Remove the tough stems of the mustard leaves. Peel the thick fibres and chop finely along with the flowers, spinach and bathua. Finely chop the green chillies; grate the ginger. Pressure cook mustard leaves, spinach, bathua with the green chillies, ginger, turmeric, jaggery and salt for 5-7 minutes. Cool. Open the cooker and add the cornmeal. Churn well using a large ladle or the mixie. Cook till thick, stirring often. Heat the butter or ghee. Add the onion, ginger and chilli powder. When the onions turn brown, add the cooked mustard greens mixture. Let it come to a boil. It should be thick and creamy. Serve hot with extra butter; if desired. Goes well with makki ki roti.

ALU KI SABZI

Ingredients (Serves 8)

- 1 kg potatoes
- 8 green chillies
- 5 cm piece of ginger
- 2 large bunches of fresh coriander leaves
- 4 tbsp refined oil
- 3 bay leaves
- 1/4 tsp asafoetida
- 1/2 tsp fenugreek seeds
- 1 tsp turmeric powder
- 2 tsp amchur powder
- 3 tsp coriander powder
- Salt to taste
- 1 tsp freshly ground pepper
- 1 tsp garam masala powder

For Tadka

- 2 tbsp ghee
- 1/2 tsp chilli powder

Preparation

Boil and peel the potatoes. Mash the potatoes coarsely with your hands. Grind the green chillies and ginger together to a rough paste. Chop the fresh coriander. Heat the oil in a karahi. Add the bay leaves, asafoetida and fenugreek seeds. When they change colour, add ginger-green chilli paste and turmeric, mixed with a tablespoon of water. When the water dries up, add potatoes along with the amchur and coriander powders. Stir fry for 2 minutes. Add 4 cups of hot water. Cook, stirring continually till gravy is thick. Add salt, pepper, garam masala and coriander leaves. Cook for 2 minutes. Separately, heat 2 tablespoon ghee. Remove from heat. Add the chilli powder. Pour over the curry and serve hot.

Punjabi Malai Palak (Moong Dal with Spinach)

Ingredients (Serves 4)

- 100 gm moong dal
- 400 gm spinach
- 1 tbsp grated ginger
- 2 green chillies, chopped
- 1/2 tsp turmeric powder
- Salt to taste

For tempering

- 1 medium onion, chopped
- 1/2 tsp chilli powder
- 4 tbsp thick curd
- A pinch of pepper powder
- 2 tbsp ghee or butter

Preparation

Wash the dal. Wash and chop the spinach. Pressure cook the spinach, dal, ginger, green chillies, turmeric and salt with 1/2 lt of water for 7 minutes. Mash well with a ladle so that everything is well mixed. Heat the ghee. Fry the onions till pink. Add the chilli powder. Fry once more and add the dal mix. Cook on high heat for 5 minutes. Add the well beaten curd and pepper. Simmer till well blended and the mixture is thick like cream. Goes well with rice as well as chappatis.

Variation: Add 1/2 cup cream before removing, particularly if you're cooking for company.

Maharashtrian Sambhar

Ingredients (Serves 6)

- 1 cup arhar dal
- 1/2 cup shelled peanuts
- 1 large brinjal
- 2 medium potatoes
- 2 tomatoes
- A small piece of pumpkin
- 10 okras
- 1 tbsp thick tamarind pulp
- Salt to taste

For Tadka

- 1 tbsp refined oil
- 1/2 tsp mustard seeds
- A few curry leaves
- A pinch of asafoetida

Roast and powder

- 1 tbsp coriander seeds
- 1/2 tsp cumin seeds
- 5 peppercorns
- 1/4 tsp fenugreek seeds
- 1 tbsp gram dal
- 1 tbsp urad dal
- 6 dry red chillies
- 1/4 tsp turmeric powder

Preparation

Boil the dal with peanuts, salt and 4 cups of water in the pressure cooker for 7 minutes. Clean and cut the vegetables into small cubes. Add to the cooked dal and simmer till done. Heat the oil in a degchi. Add the mustard seeds, asafoetida and curry leaves. As they sizzle, add the powdered spices and fry for 2 minutes on medium heat. Add the dal, tamarind pulp and more water, if needed. Simmer for 15 minutes. The sambhar must not be too thick. Serve hot with boiled rice, a dry vegetable curry, potato chips and fried papads.

Variation: Add vegetables like drumsticks, gourd and cluster beans etc.

Snacks

Methi Biscuits

Usually children refuse to eat fenugreek leaves because of the bitterness. But they'll never say no to the biscuits. Just try and see.

Ingredients (Makes 12-15 biscuits)

- 1/4 cup fresh fenugreek leaves
- 1/4 cup fresh coriander leaves
- 1 cup flour
- 1 cup atta
- A pinch of turmeric
- 1/2 tsp salt
- 1/2 tsp pepper powder
- 1/2 tsp amchur or chaat masala powder
- 1 tbsp thick curd

Preparation

Pick only the leaves of fenugreek and coriander; chop finely. This should measure 1/4 cup each. Sieve the flour, atta, turmeric, salt and baking powder together. Mix in the sugar. Beat the butter and add to the flour along with the remaining ingredients. Form into a soft dough. If needed, add a teaspoon of milk. Divide the dough into 2 parts. Roll each part between 2 sheets of grease proof paper to 1 cm thickness. Make holes with a fork on each biscuit. Cut into desired shapes. Gather the remaining dough into a ball. Roll and cut again. Place on greased and floured baking tray. Bake in an oven preheated to 350°F/ 160°C for 15-20 minutes.

Variation: You may add 1/4 cup of grated cheese for additional nutrition.

VEGETABLE PANROLIS

Ingredients (Makes 8-10)

For Pancake

- 1 egg
- 120 gm flour
- 1/4 tsp salt
- 150 ml milk

For Filling

- 2 medium potatoes
- 1 large carrot
- 1 capsicum
- 100 gm green peas
- 2 medium onions
- 2 green chillies
- 2 cm piece of ginger
- 4 cloves garlic
- Salt to taste
- A pinch of pepper
- A pinch of chilli powder
- 1/4 tsp garam masala powder
- 1 tbsp lime juice

For Batter

- 2 eggs
- 1/2 tsp garam masala powder
- 1/2 tsp sugar
- Pinch of salt
- 1/2 tsp lime juice
- Breadcrumbs as required
- Refined oil for frying

Preparation

Pancake: Separate the egg. Sieve the flour and salt together. Mix the egg yolk, flour and milk to make a smooth batter. Let it stand for an hour. Beat the egg white till stiff and fold into the batter at the time of frying. Heat a frying pan, non-stick one is preferred. Smear with just a teaspoon of oil. Pour 1/4 cup of batter and swirl the pan in a circular motion so the pancake takes a round shape. Fry over a medium heat till the unde side is golden. Take out; do not fry the other side. Prepare all the pancakes likewise.

Filling: Peel and dice the potatoes, carrots and capsicum into very small pieces. Shell peas, chop the onion and green chillies. Grate ginger and garlic.

Sweet Potato Gulab Jamun

Shakahari Kababs & Matarshuti Cutlet

Methi Paratha

Baked Puri

MIX&MATCH

Heat the oil in a karahi, add onion and saute till a light brown. Add ginger, garlic, all the vegetables, salt, pepper and chilli powder. Fry over a high heat till the moisture evaporates. Add just enough water to cook the vegetables. Cook till tender and dry. Add garam masala and lime juice. Mix well and set aside.

Batter: Beat the eggs and add seasonings.

To Serve: Take a pancake, fried side up. Fill with a little vegetable mixture and roll like a swiss roll. Seal the sides with a little flour paste. Dip in the egg batter and coat with breadcrumbs. Deep fry in oil till golden. Serve hot accompanied by chutney and salad.

Bread and Corn Supreme

Ingredients (Serves 6)

- 12 slices bread
- 1 cup corn
- 1 small capsicum
- 1 spring onion
- 1 cup thick white sauce
- Salt and pepper to taste
- 1 tsp vinegar
- 1 cup cold milk
- 1/2 cup grated cheese

For Sauce

- 1/2 cup tomato puree
- 1/2 cup cream
- 1 tbsp flour
- 2 tsp sugar
- Salt and pepper to taste

Preparation

Cut the bread slices into rounds. Boil the corn. Chop the capsicum and spring onion. Mix the white sauce, corn, capsicum, spring onion, salt, pepper and vinegar. Divide into 6 portions. Dip each round of bread in milk. Place one portion of the filling on one bread; cover with another. Prepare 6 sandwiches this way. Grease a baking dish and place the sandwiches. Pour over the remaining milk. Mix all the ingredients for the sauce. Cook over a medium heat till thick. Spread the sauce over the bread. Sprinkle the cheese on top and bake in an oven preheated to 180°C for 25-30 minutes.

Variation: Use cooked minced meat or prawns in the filling.

STUFFED CAPSICUM

Ingredients (Serves 4)

- 4 large capsicums
- 2 cm piece of ginger
- 4 cloves of garlic
- 2 medium potatoes
- 2 green chillies
- A few springs of fresh coriander leaves
- 3 large onions
- 400 gm fish, like rohu, bhetki, surmai
- 1 tbsp refined oil
- 4 tbsp tomato ketchup
- Salt to taste
- 2 tsp pepper powder

Preparation

Wash and halve the capsicums vertically. Discard the stems. Finely chop the pith and seeds. Reserve. Grind the onion, ginger and garlic together. Boil, peel and mash the potatoes. Chop the green chillies and coriander. Boil the fish in a little water. Remove the skin and bones. Heat the oil in skillet, non-stick one is preferred. Add the onion paste and capsicum seeds. Fry, stirring well till it starts to change colour. Add the fish, potatoes, green chillies, coriander leaves, salt and pepper. Fry over a medium heat for 4-5 minutes, stirring well. Add the tomato ketchup. Mix well and remove. Lightly grease a baking dish. Fill the stuffing into the capsicum halves equally. Grease the outside of the capsicums lightly. Also, smear the filling with a few drops of oil. Bake at 170°C in an oven for half an hour. Serve hot on a bed of shredded lettuce and carrots.

Variation: Use paneer, prawns or minced meat for filling. Can also be served as a side dish. It is considered a low colorie healthy snack.

Stuffed Khandavi

Ingredients (Serves 4)

For Stuffing

- 3/4 cup shelled green peas
- 3/4 cup pulpy paneer
- 1 tsp ginger-green chilli paste
- 1 tsp lime juice
- 1 tsp sugar
- Salt to taste
- 1 tbsp refined oil

For tempering

- 2 tsp refined oil
- 2 tsp each mustard, cumin and sesame seeds
- 2 dry red chillies
- A pinch of asafoetida
- 2 sprigs curry leaves

For Khandavi

- 2 cm piece of ginger
- 6 green chillies
- 1 cup curd
- $1^1/_2$ cups water
- 1 cups gramflour
- 1/4 tsp turmeric powder
- 1/2 tsp salt

Preparation

Stuffing: Grind the peas. Mash the paneer. Heat the oil in a skillet, non-stick preferred. Put in the green pea paste. Stir fry for 2-3 minutes or till the raw smell disappears. Add all the other ingredients. Fry till the moisture almost evaporates and the mixture is well blended. Remove and set aside.

Khandavis: Grind the ginger and green chilli together. Beat the curd along with the water. Mix all the other ingredients. Put in a bowl and steam in a pressure cooker for exactly 3 whistles. Open cooker after 5 minutes. In the meantime, grease the reverse side of 2 large thaalis lightly. Or, you can use a sheet of polythene or your marble topped kitchen counter. Grease them also. With a flat spoon spread the gramflour mixture quickly and evenly into a semi thick layer. Spread the filling evenly over this. Cut into strips. Roll each strip from the end nearest to you. Keep on a flat serving tray.

Tempering: Heat the oil in a small frying pan. Add all the spices. When they stop spluttering, pour over the khandvi rolls. Garnish with grated coconut and chopped coriander leaves. Can be served hot or cold with coconut chutney.

This Gujarati farsan *(snack) is a slimmers' joy, since hardly any oil is used. So all those of you who avoid fried snacks can eat your fill and not feel guilty later on.*

KACHCHE KELE KE SEEKH KABAB (RAW BANANA SEEKH KABAB)

Ingredients (Serves 4)

For Kabab

- 2 large raw bananas
- 1/3 cup paneer
- 2 cm piece of ginger
- 2 green chillies
- A few sprigs of green coriander leaves
- 2 slices of bread
- A pinch of chaat masala
- Salt to taste
- A pinch each of chilli and garam masala powders

For Batter

- 100 gm cornflour
- 2 tsp flour
- A pinch of shahjeera
- A pinch of black salt
- Refined oil for deep frying

Preparation

Parboil the bananas until just done. Peel and cool. Grate the bananas, paneer and ginger; crumble the bread slices. Chop the green chillies and coriander. Mix all the kabab ingredients to form a thick paste. Form kababs on skewers and cook in an oven or a tandoor. The oven should be preheated to 350°F/170°C till golden brown. Remove from skewers and set aside to cool.

Batter: Make a thick batter with all the ingredients except oil. Dip kababs in batter and deep fry in hot oil till crisp. Serve hot with a chutney.

Shakahari Kabab (Vegetarian Kabab)

Ingredients (Serves 6)

- 3 large green bananas
- 3 large potatoes
- 2 sweet potatoes
- 4 green chillies
- 10 cm piece of ginger
- 1 small bunch green coriander leaves
- Salt to taste
- 2 tsp white pepper powder
- 2 tbsp cornflour
- 2 tsp chaat masala
- Refined oil for frying

For Filling

- 1/3 cup hung curd
- 24 raisins

Preparation

Boil the green bananas, potatoes and sweet potatoes till just done. Do not overboil and do not pressure cook either. Peel and grate. Chop the green chillies, ginger and coriander. Mix with the grated vegetables, salt, white pepper, chaat masala and cornflour. Mash with hands till smooth. Mix the hung curd and raisins together and divide into 12 parts. Divide the mashed vegetables into 12 parts as well. Stuff each part with 1 portion of the filling; shape into tikias.Heat oil in a non-stick skillet. Shallow fry 2-3 kababs at a time till both the sides are golden. Serve hot with chutney.

Roasted Capsicum and Babycorn Chaat

Ingredients (Serves 6)

- 2 large capsicums
- 200 gm babycorns
- 100 gm onions
- 2 green chillies
- 1 large tomato
- 1 tbsp finely chopped fresh coriander leaves
- 1 tsp chopped mint leaves
- 2 tbsp refined oil

For Sauce

- 2 tbsp thick tamarind pulp
- 1 tsp jaggery
- 1/2 tsp black salt
- 1/2 tsp roasted and powdered cumin seeds

Preparation

Roast the capsicum. To do this hold the capsicum with a fork over gas flame; rotate often till the skin picks up black spots and gets somewhat charred. Take off the fire and keep it covered for 15 minutes. Repeat the process with the other one. The capsicums will sweat and this facilitates the removal of the skin. Discard the skin and seeds and cut into strips. If the babycorns are not tender, boil in salted water till soft. When cooked, cut into strips. Slice the onions into fine julliennes. Finely chop the green chillies. Discard the seeds of the tomatoes and cut into strips. Combine all the ingredients for the sauce till the jaggery is melted. Combine all the vegetables, sauce and oil. Chill and serve.

Variation: Use different coloured capsicums for better visual effect.

Cheese Pakora with Mexican Salsa

Ingredients (Serves 4)

- 16 large spinach leaves
- 200 gm cheese
- Chilli powder and amchur as needed
- Refined oil for frying

For Batter

- 100 gm flour
- 1/2 tsp baking powder
- Salt to taste

For Salsa

- 2 large tomatoes
- 1 red capsicum
- 1 green capsicum
- 1 medium onion
- 1 small cucumber
- 2 tbsp lime juice
- 2 tbsp chopped fresh coriander leaves
- 2 green chillies
- 1/2 cup tomato puree
- Salt and pepper to taste

Preparation

Take only the spinach leaves. Discard the stems. Trim each leaf into a rectangular shape. Blanch for 5 secs in hot water and pat dry. Cut the cheese into 16 thin finger shapes. Keep aside.

Batter: Sift the flour, salt and baking powder together. Add enough water to make a thick batter. Refrigerate for half an hour.

Salsa: Blanch, deseed and finely chop the tomatoes. Deseed and finely chop both the capsicums. Chop onion and green chilli Peel and chop the cucumber. In the bowl combine the tomato, capsicum, onion, lime juice, green chillies, cucumber, fresh coriander, salt and pepper. Blend 1 cup of the above tomato mixture and the tomato puree in a blender rather coarsely. Add the remaining mixture. Chill.

Place a cheese finger over a spinach leaf; sprinkle a very small pinch of chilli powder and amchur. Cover with the leaf totally. Dip in the prepared batter and deep fry till golden brown. Serve with the salsa.

Matarshuti Cutlet (Green Pea Cutlet)

Ingredients (Makes 16)

- 500 gm potatoes
- $1^1/_2$ tbsp cornflour
- $1^1/_2$ tbsp rice flour
- Salt to taste
- Poppy seeds as needed for coating
- Refined oil for frying

For Filling

- $1^1/_2$ cups shelled peas
- 2 green chillies
- 10 cashewnuts
- 15 raisins
- 1 grated ginger
- 1 tbsp refined oil
- 1/2 tsp cumin seeds
- 1/2 tsp chaat masala powder
- 1 tsp sugar
- Black salt to taste
- 1/2 tsp garam masala powder

Preparation

Boil, peel and grate the potatoes. Mash smoothly adding cornflour, rice flour and salt. Divide into 16 parts. Keep aside. Boil the peas and mash coarsely, chop the green chillies, cashewnuts and raisins. Grate the ginger. Heat the oil in a karahi and add cumin seeds. When they crackle, add peas and the remaining ingredients except chaat masala and garam masala powder. Stir fry for 5 minutes till everything gets well mixed. Sprinkle chaat masala and garam masala. Divide the mixture for the filling into 16 portions. Take one part of the potato. Shape into a cup; put one portion of the filling, close and shape into patties. Coat with poppy seeds. Shallow fry on a tawa using oil, until evenly browned.

Green Chana Tikia with Green Mango Chutney

Ingredients (Makes 15-16 Tikias)

- 500 gm green chana
- 200 gm potatoes
- 1 small bunch fresh coriander
- 4 green chillies
- 5 cm piece of ginger
- A pinch of asafoetida
- Salt to taste
- 1 tsp cumin seeds
- 1 tsp fennel seeds
- Refined oil for frying

For Chutney

- 2 tbsp fenugreek seeds
- 250 gm raw mangoes
- 1 tbsp refined oil
- 1/2 tsp rai
- 1/2 tsp cumin seeds
- 1/2 tsp aniseeds
- A pinch of salt
- A pinch of chilli powder
- 1 cup sugar or to taste
- 1/2 tsp garam masala

Preparation

Pick the green chana. Boil the chana and potatoes. Mash well together. Finely chop the green coriander. Grind the green chillies and ginger to a paste. Heat 2 tablespoon oil in a karahi. Add the asafoetida, cumin seeds and aniseeds. Add the potato mix and fry lightly. Remove from heat; add ginger-green chilli; paste, coriander leaves and salt. Form into tikias; shallow fry on a hot tawa using oil as needed.

Chutney: Soak the fenugreek seeds overnight in a cup of water. Boil in the same water till soft and strain. Peel and slice the mangoes thinly. Heat the oil in a karahi, season with rai, cumin and aniseeds. When they stop spluttering, add the mango slices, boiled fenugreek seeds, salt and chilli. Stir for 1 minute and add 1 cup of water. When the mango softens, add the sugar. Let it cook till thick. Sprinkle garam masala powder and remove.

Serve cold in a glass bowl along with hot green chana tikias.

KHEERE KA CHILLA (CUCUMBER PANCAKE)

Ingredients (Makes 12-15)

- 200 gm cucumber
- 150 gm tomatoes
- 1/4 cup fresh coriander leaves, chopped
- 1 tbsp grated ginger
- 1 green chilli
- 15-20 curry leaves
- 250 gm gramflour
- Salt to taste
- 1/4 tsp chilli powder
- Refined oil for frying

Preparation

Peel and grate the cucumber. Squeeze to get rid of some part of the moisture. Blanch the tomatoes and puree in the mixie. Strain. Grind together fresh coriander leaves, ginger and green chilli. Finely chop the curry leaves. Sieve the gramflour and add all the ingredients except oil. Mix well. If you find the batter rather thin, add a little more gramflour. Heat a tawa, non-stick is preferred. Add 2 tablespoon of the batter at a time. Fry both the sides with a little oil till golden.

Variation: Use green peas, corn, green chana or the same way. Boil them and coarsely mash. Grate cauliflower and use.

GREEN CHILLI PAKODA

Ingredients (Makes 12 Pakodas)

- 12 large green chillies
- Refined oil for deep frying

For Filling

- 2 large potatoes
- 200 gm paneer
- 1 large onion
- 6 cashewnuts
- 10 raisins
- 2 tsp chaat masala
- Salt to taste
- 1 tsp ginger-green chilli paste
- 1/2 tsp garam masala powder
- 1 tbsp refined oil

For Batter

- $1\frac{1}{2}$ cups gramflour
- 1/3 cup rice flour
- 1/2 tsp salt
- A pinch each of chilli and turmeric powders
- 1/4 tsp bicarbonate of soda
- 2 tbsp finely chopped fresh coriander leaves

Preparation

Use the large and fat green chillies meant for pickles. Slit, but do not cut through. Discard the seeds.

Filling: Boil and grate the potato. Grate the paneer also. Finely chop the onion. Heat the oil and saute onion slices till soft. Add all the ingredients and fry, stirring continuously for 5 minutes, till everything is well mixed.

Batter: Sieve all the dry ingredients. Make a batter of pakoda consistency with enough water. Add fresh coriander leaves and 2 tablespoon hot oil. Stuff the green chillies with the filling. Dip in the batter and deep fry. Serve hot with sweet sour chutney.

Variation: Use any filling of your choice like prawns, mince, fish, chicken. But the filling should be spicy.

Salads

Garden Salad

Ingredients (Serves 4)

- 2 cups broccoli florets
- 1 large carrot
- 2 ribs celery
- 4 lettuce leaves
- 1 tbsp finely chopped parsley

For Dressing

- 1/4 cup cream
- 1/2 cup mayonnaise
- 1 tbsp grated cheese

Preparation

Cut the broccoli florets into small pieces. Steam till crisp, yet tender. Scrape, parboil and thinly slice the carrot. Dice the celery ribs. You can prepare the vegetables 24 hours ahead. Cover and refrigerate.

Dressing: Beat the cream till soft peaks form. Gently fold into the mayonnaise. Mix in the cheese.

Before serving pour the dressing over the chilled vegetables. Toss to coat. Line four individual salad plates with lettuce leaves. Divide the salad equally over the lettuce lined plates. Garnish with parsley.

Variation: Use cauliflower in place of broccoli or a combination of the two.

TANDOORI SALAD

Ingredients (Serves 4)

- 250 gm paneer
- 4 rings canned pineapple
- 2 large capsicums
- 10-12 cherry tomatoes or 4 large tomatoes
- 1 large onions
- Chaat masala as needed

For Marinade

- 1/2 cup hung curd
- 1/2 cup cream
- 1 tsp black salt
- 1 tbsp lime juice
- 1 tbsp groundnut oil
- 1 tsp chaat masala
- 1 tsp roasted and powdered cumin

Preparation

Cut the paneer and pineapple into cubes. Deseed and cut the capsicum into square pieces. Keep the cherry tomatoes whole; but if using large tomatoes, quarter them. Quarter the onion and divide into sections containing two peels each. Combine all the ingredients of the marinade and beat lightly to mix. Skewer the cubed ingredients one after another. Do not make the skewer too long. You'll need 6 skewers. Use bamboo ones. Marinate the skewered vegetables for about an hour. Cook in a tandoor or over an open flame or grill in an oven, basting with the marinade till the veggies are crisp, tender and the edges somewhat charred. Serve hot or at room temperature sprinkled with the chaat masala.

Variation: Use other vegetables like baby corn, mushrooms, cauliflorets or boiled baby potatoes. If using metal skewers, then marinate the vegetables and skewer just before cooking.

Gala Cole Slaw

Ingredients (Serves 4)

- 1 medium carrot
- 500 gm cabbage
- 1/4 raisins
- 2 tbsp mayonnaise
- 2 tbsp thick curd
- 1 tsp lime juice
- 1/4 tsp sugar
- Salt and pepper to taste

Preparation

Scrape, wash and grate the carrot. Take the inner portion of the cabbage. Wash and shred finely. Wash the raisins. Combine the carrot and cabbage in a bowl. Mix the mayonnaise and curd till smooth. Stir in the lime juice, sugar, salt and pepper. Fold the dressing into the cole slow, mixing thoroughly. Chill and serve. Garnish with the raisins.

Variation: A combination of red and green cabbage may be used. May also add 1/3 cup of chopped sausages, ham, hardboiled eggs or cooked chicken.

Som Tam
(Thai Raw Papaya Salad)

Ingredients (Serves 6)

- 1 medium raw papaya
- 2 large tomatoes
- 4 green chillies
- 1/4 cup fresh coriander leaves
- 4 yard long beans (barbati)
- 1 cup roasted peanuts
- 2 tbsp brown sugar or jaggery
- 1 tbsp soya sauce
- Salt to taste
- Juice of 2 limes

Preparation

Peel and grate the papaya. It should measure 2 cups. Chop the tomatoes, green chillies and coriander. Chop the yard long beans finely. Crush the peanuts coarsely. Take a large steel bowl and pound the green chilli in it. Add the beans, papaya, and peanuts (reserve 1 tablespoon for garnishing), in that order, pounding lightly after each addition. The vegetables should be roughly crushed and not beaten to a pulp. Mix in the lime juice, salt, brown sugar or jaggery and soya sauce. Put the mixture in a glass bowl. Add tomatoes and mix well, garnish with more chopped coriander and peanuts.

Variation: 1/2 cup of grated coconut may be added. Non-vegetarians may use Nam Pla (Thai fish sauce) instead of soya sauce.

CHUTNEYS

TOMATO CHUTNEY

Ingredients (Serves 12-15)

- 2 kg tomatoes
- 2 green chillies
- 1 tsp mustard oil
- 1 tbsp grated ginger
- A pinch of salt
- 1/4 tsp chilli powder
- 750 gm sugar or to taste
- 1/3 cup chopped fresh coriander leaves
- Juice of 1 lime

Preparation

Wash and quarter the tomatoes. Chop the green chillies. Heat the oil in a karahi. Add the grated ginger and green chillies. When they emit their aroma, put in the tomatoes and salt. Stir a few times. Cover and let cook. When the tomatoes come to a boil, uncover and add the chilli powder. Cook on high heat, stirring continually, till the water released by the tomatoes dries up considerably and the tomatoes are reduced to a pulp. Add the sugar and cook, stirring frequently. Let the chutney thicken to a jam-like consistency. Be careful, because the chutney splatters badly while stirring at this stage. Remove from fire and add the coriander and lime juice. Keeps well for at least a fortnight if refrigerated.

Variation: May add a handful of raisins and 12-15 dates along with the tomatoes. Omit ginger and green chillies. Temper with mustard seeds and 2 whole dry chillies. Sprinkle with 1 teaspoon roasted and powdered panch phoran.

Walnut and Pea Chutney

Ingredients (Serves 8-10)

- 4 whole walnuts, shelled
- 1/2 cup shelled peas
- A small piece of ginger
- 2 green chillies
- 1/2 tsp cumin seeds
- 1/4 tsp chilli powder
- 2 tbsp thick curd
- 2 tsp lime juice
- 1/4 tsp salt
- 1 tsp sugar
- 1 tsp ghee
- 1/2 tsp mustard seeds

Preparation

Soak the walnut in hot water for 10 minutes. Remove the thin brown skin as much as you can. Grind walnuts to a paste. Separately, parboil the peas and grind to a paste. Grind together the ginger, green chillies, cumin seeds. Mix in chilli powder. Beat the curd till smooth. Mix the lime juice, sugar and salt. Mix with the ground walnuts and peas. Heat the ghee. Temper with the mustard seeds. When they stop popping, add to the curd mixture. Mix well. Chill and serve.

Variation: Radish can be made into chutney the same way.

Tarkarir Ambal
(Vegetable Chutney)

This chutney tastes really delicious. Add jaggery to your taste; according to how sweet or sour you want the chutney to be.

Ingredients (Serves 10-12)

- 100 gm potatoes
- 100 gm sweet potatoes
- 100 gm brinjal
- 100 gm radish
- 100 gm small baris
- 1 tbsp mustard oil
- 1/2 tsp whole mustard seeds
- A pinch of salt
- A pinch of turmeric
- 2 green chillies
- Chopped jaggery to taste
- 1 cup of tamarind juice

Preparation

Peel the potatoes and sweet potatoes. Cut all the vegetables into small cubes. Lightly fry the baris. Heat the oil in a karhai. Temper with the mustard seeds. When they pop, add the vegetables, salt, turmeric and green chillies, chopped. Stir a few times. Add 1 cup of water and the jaggery. Let it cook on medium high heat. When the vegetables are done and almost no water left, add the tamarind juice; add the baris. The vegetables will never cook properly, if tamarind is added at the beginning. Remove when a thick gravy remains.

Variation: Omit tamarind and add 1/2 kg of khatta palak, chopped.

Peper Plastic Chutney (Raw Papaya Chutney)

Ingredients (Serves 10)

- 1 kg green papaya
- 1/2 tsp edible lime
- 250 gm sugar
- 1 tsp grated ginger
- A pinch of salt
- Juice of 5 lemons

Preparation

Wash, peel, discard the seeds and cut the papaya in large wedges. Grate these, using the largest hole of the grater. Soak the papayas in water mixed with the edible lime (the kind used in paan) for about an hour. Wash thoroughly. Pressure cook the papaya without water for 2 minutes. Strain. Prepare a sugar syrup with the sugar and 3/4 cup of water. Let the syrup thicken slightly. Add ginger, papaya and salt. Let it cook over high heat till very little water is left. Remove from the fire. Add the lime juice. Cool and serve.

Variation: Use 1/2 cup of thick tamarind pulp and jaggery the same way. Omit lime juice and sugar. Sprinkle 1 teaspoon roasted and powdered paanch phoran. Lauki, diced small can be cooked the same way. Also wax gourd (petha).

The dish is so called because the papaya bits do look like small transparent plastic pieces. I have seen my mother painstakingly cutting the raw papayas into fine square pieces that's almost seethrough. Now, time and patience both being at a premium, I prefer to grate the papaya.

PICKLES

YAM PICKLE

Ingredients (Makes 2 jars of pickle)

- 1 kg yam
- $2^1/_2$ tbsp salt
- 5 tbsp paanch-phoran
- 6 tbsp mustard seeds
- 2 tbsp turmeric powder
- $1^1/_2$ tbsp chilli powder
- 1 tsp asafoetida powder
- 500 ml + 8 tbsp mustard oil

Preparation

Peel and cut the yam into 1 m thick and 3 cm x 3 cm slices. Parboil till just done. Strain and smear with salt; keep in sun for 2 hours. Grind the mustard seeds to a coarse powder. Mix all the spices and 8 tablespoon oil with the yam and again keep in the sun for a day. Put the yam pieces along with the spices in clean, dry glass or earthenware jars. Top with mustard oil. The yam pieces should be completely immersed in oil. Keep in the sun for 7 days. This pickle keeps for a long time and matures with age.

Mixed Vegetable Pickle

Ingredients (Makes 1 kg of pickle)

- 400 gm carrots
- 400 gm cauliflower
- 200 gm turnip
- 1 cup shelled peas
- 25 gm tamarind
- 50 gm jaggery
- 50 gm ginger
- 50 gm garlic (optional)
- 250 gm mustard oil
- 5 tbsp mustard seed, powdered
- $3^1/_2$ tbsp chilli powder
- 3 tbsp powdered pepper
- $4^1/_2$ tbsp salt
- 1 cup malt vinegar

Preparation

Peel and cut the vegetables in small cubes. Put them in boiling water and cook for 5 minutes. Keep covered for 5 minutes off gas. Strain well and spread on a tray. Keep in sun for 2 hours. Soak the tamarind in 1/2 cup of water and strain. Powder the jaggery. Finely slice the ginger and garlic, if using. Heat the oil and fry the ginger-garlic till light brown. Remove form fire and add all the ingredients, except jaggery. Add the jaggery when cool. Mix well. Store in sterilised jars, keep in sun for 7 days. Always use a dry spoon to take out the pickle. Even a drop of moisture will cause fungus. Use 2 tablespoon Kashmiri chilli powder for colour.

Chinese Dishes

Chinese cuisine makes optimum use of vegetables. From lotus leaves, lotus stems, mustard greens, spinach, bamboo shoots, bean sprouts to the more common vegetables like carrots, peas, beans, cauliflower, cabbage, potatoes, brinjals–all are used in combination with mutton, chicken, fish or prawns. And of course, by themselves.

Made into soups, different types of rice dishes, noodles, main dishes, snacks–you see the presence of vegetables everywhere. That's why chinese dishes constitute one of the most nutritious and balanced meals ever.

Lung Fung Soup

Ingredients (Serves 4)

- 1/2 cups bean sprouts
- 1 small carrot
- 8 French beans
- 1 large capsicum
- 1 tbsp refined oil
- 1 cup shredded cabbage
- 1/2 cup shelled peas
- 1/2 cup small cauliflorets
- 5 cups chicken stock
- Salt and white pepper to taste
- 1 tsp light soya sauce
- Pinch of monosodium glutamate
- 1 tbsp cornflour
- 2 eggs

Preparation

Wash the bean sprouts. Peel and cut the carrot into thin slices on the slant. String and dice the French beans. Deseed and dice the capsicum. Heat the oil in a large saucepan and stir fry all the vegetables over high heat for 2 minutes. Add 4 cups stock, salt, white pepper, soya sauce and monosodium glutamate; let it cook on medium high heat for 5 minutes. Mix the cornflour with remaining 1 cup stock and add to the soup stirring well. Cook for 1 minute. Beat the eggs. Remove the soup from the heat. Add the beaten eggs through a strainer and stir well so that the eggs form threads. Serve at once.

Variation: Use vegetable stock for a vegetarian version. Use any other vegetable like spinach, mustard greens, baby corn, broccoli etc.

Chicken Congee

Ingredients (Serves 4)

- 5 cups of water
- 150 gm pieces of chicken
- 1 cm piece of ginger, finely sliced
- 1 spring onion
- 2 cups rice, preferably small grained
- A pinch of salt
- Pinch of monosodium glutamate
- 4 eggs
- 4 tsp light soya sauce
- 4 tsp sesame oil

Preparation

Bring 5 cups of water to the boil; boil the chicken until well done. Debone and cut into 1 cm cubes. Strain the stock. Cut the spring onion into 5 cm sections alongwith a little of the green tops. Wash the rice well; put in a large saucepan with the stock and water to make upto 10 cups of liquid. Bring to a boil, then reduce heat. Cook for about 30 minutes, stirring from time to time. Season with salt and monosodium glutamate. Add the chicken and cook for a further 10-15 minutes. By this time the mixture should resemble a thick soup. Place an egg in each individual soup bowls, top with a few strips of ginger and spring of ginger and spring onions, 1 teaspoon soya sauce and 1 teaspoon sesame oil. Pour the boiling rice into the bowls and serve immediately.

Congee rice is a Chinese national standby equally popular at breakfast, lunch or dinner. There are various types of congees, with chicken as in this recipe—or more luxuriously with prawns, crabs and abalone.

Rice in Arbi Leaf

Ingredients (Serves 6)

- $1^1/_2$ cups long grained rice
- 200 gm chicken
- 100 gm prawns
- 1 cup shelled peas
- 1 carrot diced small
- 6 arbi leaves
- 4 tbsp refined oil
- Pinch of monosodium glutamate
- 1 tsp salt
- 1 tbsp soya sauce

Preparation

Cook the rice. It will yield approximately $4^1/_2$ cups of boiled rice. Cook the chicken; debone and chop coarsely, devein and cook the prawns. Parboil the peas and carrots. Wash the arbi leaves; pat dry and brush the insides with a little oil. Heat 1 tablespoon oil in a non-stick skillet and stir-fry the chicken and prawn for 1 minute. Remove. Heat the remaining oil in a karahi, stir-fry the rice until it is well coated with oil and heated through. Add the chicken, prawns, peas, carrot, soya sauce, monosodium glutamate and salt. Divide the rice equally in between the arbi leaves. Fold the leaves over the rice, enclosing in neat packages. Steam for 15 minutes. You can use a pressure cooker, in that case don't use the weight. Or, a rice cooker or dhokla steamer may also be used.

The Chinese use lotus leaves. I have substituted arbi leaves for convenience and easy availability.

Five-Colour Rice

Ingredients (Serves 4)

- 50 gm ham
- 100 gm cooked chicken
- 2 eggs
- 6 tbsp refined oil
- 100 gm cooked prawns
- 2 tbsp shelled peas
- 2 tbsp diced carrots
- 2 tbsp diced French beans
- 2 tbsp cauliflorets
- 2 tbsp diced red capsicum
- 2 tbsp light soya sauce
- Pinch of monosodium glutamate
- Pinch of pepper
- 2 spring onions, chopped
- 4 cups boiled rice
- 1 tsp salt

Preparation

Dice the ham and chicken into small cubes. Parboil all the vegetables, except capsicum. Beat the eggs and season with the salt and monosodium glutamate. Heat 1 tablespoon oil in a frying pan; pour in the egg and scramble. Set aside on plate. Heat 2 tablespoon oil in wok or a karahi over a high flame and add the ham, chicken, prawns, peas, carrots, beans, cauliflower and capsicum. Stir well. Once all the ingredients have heated through, pour in the soya sauce. Stir and turn, giving the soya sauce time to flavour the other ingredients and season with a pinch each of monosodium glutamate and pepper. Remove from the karahi and reserve. Clean the karahi, pour in 4 tablespoon of oil and heat; stir fry the spring onions to flavour the oil, but do not let it brown. Add the rice and stir fry over a medium heat, stirring and turning continuously taking care not to crush the rice grains. Serve with 1/2 teaspoon of salt and a pinch of monosodium glutamate. When the rice is well mixed and coated with oil, add the reserved ingredients and stir fry. Add the scrambled eggs and mix once more before serving. Serve with chopped green chillies soaked in vinegar.

The delicious Chinese dish that can be prepared quickly when you have unexpected guests.

Noodles with Mixed Vegetables

Ingredients (Serves 6)

- 2 whole boneless chicken breasts
- 6 leaves Chinese cabbage
- 1 onion
- 100 gm bean sprouts
- 1 small carrot
- 2 capsicums
- 1/2 cup shelled peas
- 1 tbsp grated ginger
- 6 small packet noodles
- 5 tbsp oil
- 3 tbsp Worcestershire sauce
- 2 tbsp soya sauce
- Salt and pepper to taste
- A pinch of monosodium glutamate

Preparation

Boil and cut the chick breasts into thin strips. Shred the chinese cabbage. Slice the onion thinly. Wash the bean sprouts and drain well. Peel and cut the carrot into thin slivers. Remove the seeds and pith of the capsicum and cut into juliennes. Boil the peas. Place the noodles in a bowl; cover with boiling water. Keep for 2 minutes. Drain. Heat 3 tablespoon oil in a karahi and stir fry the noodles over a high heat till somewhat crisp. Heat the remaining 2 tablespoon oil in a skillet. Stir fry the grated ginger and as soon as it stars to give off its aroma, add the chicken, cabbage, onion, bean sprouts, carrot, capsicum and peas. Stir fry. When the vegetables are almost done, season with the Worcestershire sauce, soya sauce, salt, pepper and monosodium glutamate. Add the noodles. Toss to mix well and heat through.

Variation: Use prawns, ham and any other vegetables of your choice.

FIVE-COLOUR OMELETTE

Ingredients (Serves 4)

- 100 gm bamboo shoots
- 4 button mushrooms
- 2 slices ham
- 2 spring onions
- 6 eggs
- 1 tsp salt
- 1/2 tsp sugar
- Pinch of monosodium glutamate
- 3 tbsp refined oil

Preparation

You can use canned or fresh bamboo shoots. If fresh ones are being used, wash well and boil until tender. Shred into small match-like strips. Slice the mushrooms thinly. Equal amount of oyster mushrooms may be used as well. Cut the ham into thin strips. Shred the spring onion into 5 cm long strips, using part of the green tops as well. Beat the eggs in a bowl. Mix in the salt, sugar, monosodium glutamate. Beat the eggs well, lifting the mixture to incorporate as much air as possible. Add the ham, spring onion, bamboo shoots and mushroom; stir well. Heat 3 tablespoon oil in a skillet. Pour the whole into it at once. Stir with a spatula to make sure the ingredients are evenly spread through. Cook until just set. When the omelette has set on one side, it should be a light golden brown in colour. Turn over, make a few slits with the spatula so that the insides get cooked. Cover and cook for 2 minutes. Take out. Cut in wedges. Serve hot with green chillies in vinegar and light soya sauce. Served with a salad, this constitutes a light meal.

Variation: May use finely shredded cooked chicken, prawn etc.

Fish with Chinese Cabbage

Ingredients (Serves 4)

- 250 gm fish fingers
- 1 tsp ginger juice
- 2 tsp sherry
- 6 large Chinese cabbage leaves
- 8 flat beans
- 1 small carrot
- 1 spring onions
- 6 button mushrooms
- 1/2 cup shelled peas
- Cornflour as required
- Refined oil for frying the fish
- $1\frac{1}{2}$ cups chicken stock
- 1/2 tsp salt
- 1/2 tsp sugar
- 1/2 cup thickened milk
- 1/4 cup cream (optional)
- 2 tsp cornflour mixed with 3-4 tsp water
- 1 tbsp refined oil

Preparation

Mix the fish fingers with the ginger juice and sherry and leave for 5 minutes. Cut the stalks of the Chinese cabbage into large pieces. Cut the green leafy part into small pieces. Trim the flat beans and remove strings. Peel the carrot and slice thinly. Chop the spring onions with most of the green part as well. Wash and slice the mushrooms. Coat the fish fingers one at a time with cornflour; shake off excess. Heat enough oil for deep frying in a karahi and deep fry the fish briefly. Heat 1 tablespoon oil in a karahi and stir fry the spring onion for 30 seconds. Add the harder, white part of the Chinese cabbage, flat beans, mushrooms, green peas, carrots and leafy part of the cabbage in that order, while stirring after each addition. Pour in the stock and cook for 5-7 minutes. As soon as the vegetables are tender, add the fish. Season with the salt and sugar. Add the thickened milk. Cook for 1 minute then stir in the cornflour to thicken. Remove from fire and add the cream, if desired to make the sauce rich and creamy.

Variation: Use prawns, cooked chicken pieces, mustard greens, spinach, baby corn, cabbage or any vegetable of your choice.

Prawn and Peas–Sichuan Style

Ingredients (Serves 6)

- 2 tbsp chilli oil
- 1/2 kg prawns
- 1 egg white
- 1 tsp cornflour
- Refined oil for frying
- 2 cups shelled peas
- 1 tsp grated ginger
- 1 tbsp sherry
- 1 tsp salt
- 1/2 tsp sugar
- 1/2 tsp pepper
- Pinch of monosodium glutamate

Preparation

To make chilli oil: Heat 1 cup of refined oil till it smokes. Take off fire and add 1tablespoon chilli powder. Cover and keep thus for a couple of hours. Strain and keep bottled. Use as directed. This oil keeps well for a long time.

Peel and devein the prawns. Wash well. Dry the prawns and mix with the egg white and cornflour. Cook the peas. Deep fry the prawns in hot refined oil, stirring well with a perforated spoon so they do not stick to one another. Drain properly. Heat the chilli oil in a karahi. Add the ginger. Once the ginger starts to release its aroma, add the peas and just allow it to cook. Add the prawns and stir fry. Pour in the sherry, salt and sugar. Season with pepper and monosodium glutamate. Stir well and remove.

MIX&MATCH
Yam & Pea Keema
Roasted Chicken with Vegetable Stuffing

Shahi Stuffed Tomato

Stuffed Capsicum

Bhindani Kadhi

Sweet and Sour Chicken

Ingredients (Serves 6)

- 1 medium onion
- 1 small capsicum
- 1 large tomato
- 1 medium cucumber
- 2 rings of canned pineapple
- 6 cauliflorets
- 1/2 cup shelled peas
- 300 gm boneless chicken
- 1 egg
- 4 tbsp flour
- 1/4 tsp baking powder
- Salt to taste
- A pinch of monosodium glutamate
- Refined oil for frying
- 1 cup chicken stock

For Sauce

- $1\frac{1}{2}$ tbsp cornflour
- 1 cup chicken stock
- 3 tbsp malt vinegar
- 3 tbsp sugar
- 3 tbsp pineapple juice
- 2 tbsp thin soya sauce
- 2 tbsp tomato ketchup
- Salt and pepper to taste

Preparation

Quarter the onions, divide into peels. Discard the seeds and cut the capsicum into square pieces. Cut the tomato into chunks. Peel and cut the cucumber into thick slices on the slant, cube the pineapple rings. Blanch cauliflorets and peas. Mix the sauce ingredients together. Cut the chicken into slices. Mix the eggs, flour, baking powder, pinch of salt, monosodium glutamate into a smooth paste. Coat the chicken pieces with it and deep fry in oil till a golden brown. Remove. Heat 2 tablespoon oil in a karahi. Stir fry the onion for 1 minute. Add the cauliflorets, peas, capsicum, cucumber, tomato and pineapple in that order—stir frying after each addition. Saute the whole thing for 2 minutes. Add the stock and fried chicken and cook for 5 minutes over a medium heat. Mix the sauce ingredients together and pour over the chicken, stir until the mixture thickens and becomes translucent.

Variation: Use prawns, meat balls, boneless pork or mutton in place of chicken. Or eschew the chicken altogether and make a vegetarian version.

Vegetable Sizzler

Preparation (Serves 4)

- 300 gm paneer
- 1 tbsp lime juice
- Salt and pepper to taste
- Flour as needed
- Refined oil for frying
- 4 pineapple slices
- 250 gm Fench beans
- 2 large carrots

Potatoes

- 8 large potatoes
- 2 heaped tbsp boiled corn kernels
- 1 tbsp chopped parsley or green coriander leaves
- 4 tbsp cream
- 2 tbsp finely chopped cashewnuts
- 2 tbsp finely chopped raisins
- A little grated cheese

Tomatoes

- 8 large tomatoes
- 1 kg spinach
- 1 tbsp butter
- 1 tsp chopped garlic
- 1 tbsp chopped onion
- Salt and pepper to taste
- Pinch of sugar
- 2 tbsp cream
- Little melted butter

Orange Sauce

- 1 cup fresh orange juice
- 2 tbps sugar
- 1 tsp cornflour

Brown Sauce

- 2 small carrots
- 1 onion
- 6 cloves of garlic
- 1 stick celery
- 50 gm beans
- 3 tbsp tomato puree
- 4 bay leaves
- 2 tbsp refined oil
- 2 tbsp flour
- 1 tomato
- 1 tbsp cream
- 1 tbsp butter

Preparation

Cut the paneer into 8 thick slices. Sprinkle lime juice, salt and pepper to taste. Lightly roll in flour and shake off excess. Fry in a little oil in a non-stick pan. Cut the pineapple slices into half. Grill in a non-stick pan without fat till a little coloured. Cut the beans into half and remove tough strings. Peel and cut carrot into fingers. Blanch both in lightly salted water. Heat 1 teaspoon butter in a non-stick pan and saute beans and carrots separately sprinkling a little salt and pepper. Keep aside.

Potato: Bake or parboil the potatoes. To bake, wash and wrap the whole potatoes in foil. Bake at 200°C in an oven for 40-45 minutes. Cut the potatoes into half, scoop out 3/4 of the centre. Save the shells. Mix the scooped cut centre with boiled corn, chopped parsley, salt, pepper, cream, cashewnuts and raisins. Stuff each potato with the prepared filling; sprinkle a little grated cheese. Bake or grill in a hot oven for 5 minutes.

Tomatoes: Slice off the top of each tomato and scoop out the seeds. Keep inverted. Take only the leaves of the spinach and wash well. Blanch in hot water for 2 minutes, then plunge them in cold water. This sets the colour. Squeeze to get rid of all water. Chop roughly. Heat the butter. Saute garlic and onion. When they start to brown–about 3 minutes, add spinach, salt and pepper. Saute for 5 minutes. Add the cream. Keep stirring well. Fill in the scooped tomatoes. Drizzle a few drops of butter on each. Bake or grill in a hot oven for 43 minutes.

Orange Sauce: Boil the orange juice and sugar together till reduced to half. Mix the cornflour with 1 tablespoon milk and pour in. Keep stirring well. Cook till the sauce thickens somewhat. Remove.

Brown sauce: Roughly chop all the vegetables. Heat the oil, temper with the bay leaves and add the vegetables. Stir fry till brown. Add the tomato puree and saute. Add the flour add stir well. Add $2^1/_2$ cups of water. Cover and cook over a medium heat till reduced by half. Discard the bay leaves. Blend and strain the sauce. Put on medium heat again, sprinkle salt and pepper. Remove from heat once it boils. Add the cream and butter, mix well.

To set up the sizzler: Heat very well 4 sizzler plates; place some cabbage leaves on them. Place on each plate 2 pieces of fried paneer and 2 pieces of pineapple. Place the stuffed vegetables on both the sides. Garnish with sauteed beans and carrots. Pat 1 tablespoon orange sauce on the paneer and 1 tablespoon brown sauce on the pineapple. Pour more of both the sauce by the sides. Place an ice cube and some butter on each of the hot sizzler plates for the desired sizzler effect and serve at once.

SWEET POTATO GULAB JAMUN

Ingredients (Makes 15)

- 1/2 kg sweet potatoes
- $1^1/_2$ tbsp flour
- A pinch of soda bicarb
- $1^1/_2$ cups sugar
- 1/2 cup khoya
- 15 pieces of misri
- Ghee or vanaspati for frying
- 1 tbsp rose water

Preparation

Boil the sweet potatoes till just done. Do not overcook. Peel and mash, discarding membranes, if any. Mix the flour and soda bicarb together and add to the potatoes. Mash again so that everything gets well mixed. Add 3/4 cup of water to the sugar and prepare a syrup, a little thinner than the one string consistency. Divide the sweet potatoes into 15 parts. Place a little khoya and 1 piece of misri in it and form a smooth round ball. Heat the ghee or vanaspati in a karahi till it smokes. Remove from fire and put in the gulab jamuns, 5 at a time. Put on heat again and fry till a golden brown. Then remove from the ghee and put in the syrup. Sprinkle rose water and keep them immersed in the syrup till serving time. Heat the gulab jamuns along with the syrup if you want to serve them hot.

Potato Halwa

Ingredients (Serves 4)

- 250 gm medium potatoes
- 100 gm cashewnuts
- 200 gm powdered sugar
- 100 gm khoya
- 125 gm pure ghee
- 1/2 tsp green cardamom powder
- 1/2 tsp nutmeg powder
- 2 tbsp finely chopped almonds and pistachios or silver foil for garnishing.

Preparation

Boil, peel and mash the potatoes till smooth. There should be no lumps. Lightly roast the cashewnuts and powder. Grate the khoya. Heat the ghee in a karahi, non-stick is preferred. Put in the mashed potatoes; add the cashewnut powder and sugar. Stir continuously over a slow fire. The potatoes will thin down at first. As you stir, it will become brownish in colour and the ghee will separate. By that time the halwa will thicken considerably. Sprinkle the powdered spice and mix well. Pour into a greased tray evenly. Decorate with the chopped almonds and pistas or silver foil. Cut into squares. Serve piping hot or cold.

Carrot Cake

Ingredients (Serves 8)

- $1\frac{1}{2}$ cups flour
- 1 tsp baking powder
- 1/2 tsp soda bicarb
- 1/2 cup chopped walnuts
- 1/2 cup raisins
- 180 gm butter
- $1\frac{1}{2}$ cups castor sugar
- 3 eggs
- 1/2 tsp grated nutmeg
- 1 tbsp grated lime rind
- $1\frac{1}{2}$ cups coarsely grated carrot
- 1/3 cup orange juice

Preparation

Sift the flour, baking powder and sode bicarb together. Mix the walnuts and raisins with the flour. Beat the butter till soft. Add the castor sugar and beat till light and fluffy. Add the eggs, one at a time, beating after each addition. Add the grated nutmeg and lime rind and beat once. Fold in the grated carrot and when properly blended, add the flour mixture, a little at a time, alternating with the orange juice and finishing with the flour. Line a baking tin with paper and grease it. Pour the cake batter into it and bake in an oven preheated to 350°F/180°C for 40 minutes. Serve warm or cold.

Carrot cake is a very soft and moist cake that keeps well. It is an excellent picnic food.

Bund Gobhi ki Rabri (Cabbage Rabri)

Ingredients (Serves 6)

- 1 lt full cream milk
- 1 cup cabbage leaves
- 125 gm sugar
- 1 tbsp ghee or white butter
- 5 drops kewra essence
- Silver leaf for decoration

Preparation

The milk must be of top quality full cream milk. Take only the inner leaves of the cabbage. Discard any tough veins and cut into rectangular pieces. Heat the ghee or butter in a frying pan and add the cabbage. Saute over a medium heat for 5 minutes. Set aside. Bring the milk to a boil in a saucepan. Add the cabbage and sugar and simmer, stirring continually at first and then more frequently till the milk is reduced by one-third. Add the kewra just before serving. Serve hot or cold, decorated with silver leaf.

Variation: Grated bottle gourd can be cooked the same way.

The dish looks and tastes like real rabri. The rectangular pieces of cabbage resemble the pieces of malai.

Green Pea Burfi

Ingredients (Makes 15-16 burfis)

- 25 pistachios
- 5 almonds
- 500 gm green peas
- 50 gm ghee
- 100 gm khoya
- 250 gm sugar
- Silver foil for garnishing

Preparation

Soak the pistachios and almonds overnight. Peel and shred the almonds in slivers. Shell and parboil the peas. Grind to a paste along with the pistachios. Grate the khoya. Heat the ghee in a karahi. Add the pea paste and fry for 5 minutes over a high heat, stirring continuously. Add the khoya and sugar. Fry till the peas leave the sides of the vessel. Pour on a greased tray. Garnish with the silver foil and slivered almonds. Cut into pieces when cool.

Carrot Kheer

Ingredients

- 2 lt full cream milk
- 4 green cardamoms
- 225 gm grated carrot
- 200 gm sugar
- A handful of raisins
- 10 cashewnuts, chopped

Preparation

Boil the milk with the green cardamoms for 15 minutes. Add the carrots, sugar, raisins and cashewnuts. Cook till thick. Can be served hot or cold.

Glossary of Food and Cooking Terms

Appetiser: Food taken before the main meal to stimulate the appetite.

Au gratin: A dish covered with sauce, bread crumbs or cheese and then baked or grilled and served in the same dish.

Baking: Cooking by dry heat in an oven.

Barbecue: To roast either whole or cut pieces of any meat on direct heat on a spit or rack. Of course, fish or vegetables can also be barbecued.

Basting: Pouring spoonfuls of melted fat over the surface of food being baked or roasted.

Batter: Mixing of flour, gramflour, cornflour or any other kind of flour with water, milk or any kind of liquid into a particular consistency.

Beating: An up and down motion with a fork or rotary beater to mix the food thoroughly and to introduce air.

Binding: Adding egg cream or melted fat to a dry mixture to hold it together.

Birishta: Thinly sliced onion fried slowly till crisp and golden brown. It is then added to a dish–used mostly in Mughlai cooking.

Bite size: Small pieces of food that can be eaten in one bite.

Blanching: Removing the outer skin after plunging it in hot water and then in cold water. Eg., blanching of almonds or tomatoes.

Blending: Mixing of two or three ingredients into a smooth paste.

Boiling: Cooking in a liquid at a temperature of 100°C.

Boning: Removing bones of meat, poultry or fish.

Bread: To cover with fresh or dry breadcrumbs completely.

Browning: Searing the outer surface of meat at high flame to seal in the juices.

Brushing: Applying an even coat of milk, egg or butter on the surface of food to get a shiny top.

Caramelise: To cook sugar till it turns golden.

Casserole: A covered ovenproof dish. Casserole cooking denotes very slow cooking in a casserole dish; excellent for meat, fish or vegetables as the food becomes very tender and the nutrients are conserved.

Chilling: Cooking food without freezing in the refrigerator.

Chop: To cut food into small pieces with a knife or blender.

Clarify: To clear or purify fat from water, stock, meat juices so that it can be used for frying, pastry making and the like.

Coat: To sprinkle food with or dip it into flour etc., until completely covered.

Colander: Perforated metal or plastic container used for draining liquid.

Combine: To mix ingredients.

Condiment: Spices and seasonings.

Consistency: The thickness or texture of a mixture.

Core: To remove the central membrane or pips etc. from fruits like apples and pears.

Creaming: Mixing two or more ingredients with a wooden spoon or mixer to make them soft and creamy.

Cube: To cut food into small cubes (about 1 cm).

Cut in: To distribute solid fat in flour using a knife or fingertips.

Cut and fold: To add an ingredient very gently to a mixture.

Degchi: A traditional vessel of straight sides and a horizontal rim.

Dice: To cut into small pieces.

Dissolve: To melt, as solid food into liquid.

Dot: To place small blobs of fat over the surface of food.

Dough: A mixture of flour, water or milk which is firm enough to knead and form into shapes.

Drain: To remove liquid from solid food.

Dress: (a) To arrange and garnish food.
(b) To pluck, draw and truss a chicken or poultry.

Dressing: A sauce used for pouring on salad before serving.

Dropping consistency: The consistency of cake and pudding mixture before cooking; if a spoonful of mixture is lifted from the bowl. It should drop off the spoon in 5 seconds.

Dusting: Sprinkling lightly with salt, pepper, flour, sugar or spices.

Fillet: Long, thin boneless piece of fish or meat.

Flake: Separate food gently with a fork (like flaking fish from bones).

Folding in: Mixing one ingredient into another normally with a spatula.

Deep frying: The food is completely immersed in fat. The pan should never be more than one-third full and never overcrowded.

Shallow frying: Fat should come halfway up the food. It should be turned over just once. The fat should be hot enough to sizzle on contact with the food so that the juices are sealed up immediately.

Garnish: Decorating a dish with something edible that adds colour and flavour.

Grate: To rub against a grater to get thin shreds.

Gravy: the resultant liquid that is left after cooking food.

Grease: To coat the surface of a dish or tin with fat to prevent sticking.

Grill: 1. To cook by direct radiant heat. 2. The appliance or part of a cooker used for this type of cooking.

Grind: To reduce hard food, such as nuts, or spices into fine particles. Grinding can be wet or dry.

Julienne: Vegetables cut in thin match-like strips.

Infuse: To extract flavour from spices and herbs by covering with boiling liquid and leaving to stand without further heating; the liquid is usually strained and the herbs or spices discarded.

Kabab: Small pieces of meat threaded on a shewer and braised or fried.

Karahi: A heavy iron pan used for deep frying and cooking. Now a days aluminium, steel or non-stick karahis are also available.

Ketchup: A sauce based on one major ingredient such as tomatoes or mushrooms, preserved with vinegar or spices.

Knead: To work dough with hands, pressing, stretching or folding until it is smooth.

Knock back: To knead proven yeast dough once again after it has risen, so as to expel accumulated air.

Kofta: Balls of fish, meat or vegetables, fried. Koftas are also curried.

Lukewarm: Just above blood heat, at about 40°C/80° F.

Marinate: To coat or soak food in certain spices or sauces for a period of time. This helps infuse flavours or, as in the case of meats, to tenderise them. The combination of spices and sauce is called marinade.

Melt: To heat and liquify.

Mince: To chop food very fine.

Monosodium glutamate: A white crystalline salt that enhances the natural flavour of food. Also known by its brand name Ajinomoto.

Paanch phoran: A mixture of equal quantities of whole nigella, mustard seeds, cumin seeds, fenugreek seeds and aniseeds. Used in Bengali cuisine extensively.

Parboil: To partially boil food.

Pare: To peel the outer covering.

Pith: The white cellular lining between the rind and flesh of a citrus fruit.

Poach: To cook egg by placing it shelled in boiling water. Or, to cook food in a simmering liquid.

Pot roast: Cooking large pieces of meat or poultry by braising.

Pressure cook: Is to drive out all the air, and thus have a very high temperature in which the food cooks, so that it is much faster. It is important to read the instructions of the pressure cooker, before use.

Prove: To let a dough rise till double in volume, in case of dough mixed with yeast.

Reduce: To reduce the volume of a liquid by rapid boiling in an open pan.

Rest: Is literally to rest a dough for a certain period of time. A term mostly used for doughs and batters.

Rinds: Of lemons or oranges are generally used to add zest to a dish. It is only the outer coloured portion of the skin of the fruit that is used.

Roast. To cook by dry heat in an oven or on an open flame.

Roux: A mixture of fat and flour cooked together to form the basis of a sauce and for thickening sauces and stews.

Rub in: Flour and fat are mixed together by rubbing with the fingertips to resemble fine breadcrumbs.

Saute: To fry food rapidly in hot fat, tossing and turning often.

Scald: Means (a) cooking in a liquid, just below boiling point. This temperature is indicated when tiny bubbles form around the edges of the pan. (b) Dipping food in boiling water.

Sear: To brown the surface of the food quickly over high heat (generally meat).

Season: To add salt, pepper or spices to food, to add its flavour.

Seasonings: Herbs and condiments used to improve the taste and appearance of food.

Shred: Cut into strips.

Sieve: To rub or press a moist food such as cooked vegetables or fruits, through a sieve.

Sift: To shake a dry ingredient through a sieve to remove lumps.

Simmer: To cook gently over low heat.

Skewer: Long metal or wooden pins used to pierce meat or fish for keeping them in place during roasting.

Skillet: A heavy shallow frying pan with slightly raised sides.

Skin: To remove scum or fat from the surface of a food.

Steam: To cook in a double boiler or in a basin standing in (but not covered by) boiling water.

Steep: To soak in liquid.

Stew: To cook slowly and for a long period, in plenty of simmering liquid. The cooking liquid may be thickened and is served with the finished dish.

Stir: To mix with a circular action.

Stir fry: To cook quickly in a little hot fat, stirring constantly.

Stock: Liquid in which meat, poultry or fish is cooked.

Strain: To strain liquids from solids, using a sieve, colander, cloth etc.

Stuffing: A savoury or sweet mixture used to fill another ingredient like chicken, potato, sweets etc.

Sweat: To cook food gently in melted fat in a covered pan until the juices run.

Syrup: A concentrated solution of sugar in water. Golden syrup is a by-product of sugar refining.

Tandoor: Cylinderical clay oven used to take and roast in Indian cuisine. Gas tandoors are now available.

Tarka/ Temper: To add whole spices into hot fat so the fat is impregnated with the flavour of the spices. An important step in Indian cooking.

Tepid: Approximately at blood heat. Tepid water is obtained by adding two parts cold water to one part boiling water.

Toast: To cook food over dry heat or under a grill to make it brown and crisp, for example toasting bread.

Toss: To mix foods lightly with a lifting motion, using two forks and spoons.

Trivet: The perforated plate used in a pressure cooker through which stream passes.

Truss: To fasten wings etc. of fowl with thread before roasting.

Whey: That part of milk which remains liquid when the rest forms curds or paneer.

Whip: To beat rapidly with fork, mixer or egg beater to introduce air so that volume is increased.

Whisk: To stir or beat very briskly; a hand or electric beater or wire whisk is used.

Wok: A chinese cooking pan similar to our karahi with a more flat base. This is the correct pan for stir frying.

Yeast: This is the raiser for bread dough. There are generally two types of yeast, fresh/compressed or dry.

Zest: Grated outer skin of citrus fruit which is used to flavour foods and liquids.

Medicinal Properties of Vegetables

Bitter gourd: Bitter gourd is high in Vitamin C, potassium, copper and iron and fair in phosphorus and sodium. It has excellent medicinal virtues. It is antidotal, antipyretic, appetising, antibilious and laxative. It has been established that it contains a substance which is like insulin that effectively lowers the sugar level in diabetics. Bitter gourd juice taken with honey is effective against asthma, gout, rheumatism and jaundice.

Bottle gourd: A common vegetable in India, bottle gourd is full of minerals and vitamins. It is rich in vitamin B. The cooked vegetable is cooling, diuretic, sedative and antibilious. Gourd juice has a neutralising effect on the toxins in the blood. It also serves to remove worms from the digestive tract. It cures acidity and is good for the liver. Gourd also gives relief to swelling, prevents kidney stones and helps diabetics.

Cabbage: Of all the leafy and green vegetables, cabbage holds a special place because of its uncommon medicinal properties.

Raw cabbage is delicious, vitalizing, a little pungent, digestive and light. It is also used in the treatment of gastric disorders, cardiac irregularities, constipation, chronic cough, fever, biliousness and urinary tract problems.

Cabbage has sufficient vitamin C that can be assimilated and good iron content. Because of its high iron contents, it should be liberally used by expectant mothers and those suffering from anaemia.

Recent research has proved that cabbage contains tartaric acid, which inhibits the conversion of sugar and other carbohydrates into fat. A helping of cabbage juice or raw salad would be the simplest way to stay slim.

Carrot: No vegetable can match carrot in its food and medicinal values as well as in its versatility in use.

Carrots are high in Pro Vitamin A–Carotene. All non-green vegetables contain carotene in good amount but carrot beats them all. Carotene is essential for eye sight, maintenance and functioning of the mucous membrane of the body, the outer skin coverings and the linings of various body passages like eyes, eyelids, ear, nose, mouth, respiratory and digestive tracts.

Chewing raw carrot cleans teeth and strengthens the gums. Carrot juice is very beneficial. It is diuretic in action. It also eliminates unwanted uric acid from the blood and is, therefore, very good for gout patients.

Coriander: Fresh coriander is the perennial favourite of Indian cooking. Very few savoury dishes are let off without a garnishing of finely chopped coriander leaves.

Coriander leaves have an aroma and flavour of their own and have a cooling effect on the body and help in the digestion of food. Its high potassium, phosphorus, calcium, iron and vitamin A and B make coriander an all round marvel.

Cucumber: In the East, this trailing annual plant has been cultivated extensively for 3,000 years before it spread westwards.

When taken raw, cucumber acts as a diuretic. It is helpful in combating high pressure, toxemia or constipation. Besides it allays bile and has soothing effect. It gives relief to those with arthritis or diabetes.

Cucumber juice possesses many medicinal properties. It helps dislodge toxins. As it is low in calories, it is liked by the slimmers. It is also a valuable source of potassium, sodium, magnesium, sulphur, silicon, chlorine and fluorine.

It is also a good beauty aid as it contains natural bleach and is an astringent.

Curry leaves: No South Indian recipe is complete without these bright green leaves. These highly aromatic leaves possess the qualities of a herbal tonic. Ayurvedic medicine relies heavily on curry leaves for a number of its cures.

The leaves and the stem are used as a tonic, stimulant and carminative. Made into a paste, it cures biles and eruptions. Fresh juice of the leaves mixed with lime juice and sugar is exceptionally useful in digestive disorders and eating 10 curry leaves every morning for 3 months is said to cure hereditary diabetes. A liberal intake of curry leaves impedes premature greying of hair. The leaves, boiled in coconut oil, are massaged into the scalp to promote hair growth and check greying.

Coconut: The wonder food coconut is considered sacred in India. The true value of the coconut comes from the spectrum of food and medicine it offers to mankind. High in protein, minerals and vitamins and representing an ecosystem complete in itself, the coconut offers milk, water, cream, oil and meat for a variety of cures, from the treatment of burns, nourishment for hair growth to the treatment of kidney stones and ailment of heart and blood pressure.

Drumstick: All parts of the drumstick are used in Ayurvedic medicine. Drumsticks have been confirmed as a natural antibiotic and antifungal agent.

Nutritionally, drumstick pods, flowers and leaves are of great value as sources of acrotene, calcium, phosphorus and vitamin C.

Fresh leaf juice applied with lime juice is useful in the treatment of pimples, blackheads and keeps one's skin fresh.

Fenugreek: Fresh fenugreek leaves are extremely rich in iron, calcium, sulphur, chlorine and vitamin A and C. The leaves are highly alkaline. These leaves are highly prized for their aromatic bitterness and are extensively used in Indian cooking and have a cooling effect. They are good for digestion and help sluggish liver and lungs.

Garlic: Garlic is as old as mankind. It finds its name mentioned in *The Bible,* thereby proving its use from the very early time. Apart from the fact that it adds flavour to food, it has medicinal qualities that diminish cholesterol in the blood. It contains sulphur compounds which kill bacteria.

Garlic is used to treat asthma, leprosy, bronchial congestion, arteriosclerosis, worms and countless other ailments. Garlic oil can check high cholesterol, aid digestion or control blood pressure, rheumatism, cancerous growth and whooping cough.

Ginger: Ginger, too is a must for all good cooked food and as medicine. Ginger has been used as medicine in India from the Vedic period and is called *mahaus̀hadhi* meaning great medicine.

Ginger paste is effective against mumps and tonsils. An infusion of ginger is said to relieve sore throats and head colds. Ginger overcomes flatulence and heaviness due to overreating. Gum inflammation can be reduced by applying dry ginger powder combined with powdered pepper.

Green chillies: The most popular spice used as an ingredient in our daily dishes, chillies are found all over the world under different names.

We use chillies mainly for adding pungency and colour to our dishes. This pungency has many useful effects on our body such as anti-inflammatory and anti-obesity effects, amalgesic etc.

Chillies are very high in vitamins A and C and have more vitamin C per gram than many oranges. Capsicum preparations are used as counter irritants for lumbago and rheumatic disorders. They are also added to medicines which relieve sore throats. However, beware of over indulgence; chillies can damage the lining of the stomach.

Mint: Just as the South Indians rely heavily on curry leaves as a flavouring agent, the North Indians use mint. Indeed mint is favoured all over the world. The very mention of mint gives a cool refreshing feeling.

Mint is used to treat influenza, coughs and colds because of its sweat inducing and anti-bacterial qualities. Menthol, the oil extract from mint, is anaesthetic and is used in relieving pains in sprains and rheumatism. It is very effectively used to combat vomitting and flatulence. Chewing the leaves mitigates bad breath and comforts sore gums.

An infusion of mint sweetened with honey is a good expectorant. Mint oil is used in throat lozenges and ointment for headaches. Mint is used to flavour toothpaste, mouth wash, tobacco in menthol cigarettes, confectionary and perfumery.

Onion: Onions have, since ancient times, been considered as important as cereals for human nutrition. It is one of the oldest cultivated vegetables. It is first discussed in ancient Indian treatises as early as 600 A.D. Today they are used extensively for their flavour and medicinal value and every kitchen maintains a stack of onions.

Onions are potent antibiotics. They are expectorants and would help clear the lungs of mucus and phlegm. They are good for anaemia, cold, insomnia, nervous disorders and for stimulating circulation. Onions also possess anti-toxic properties. They also reduce blood cholesterol and their consumption is recommended for people with heart problems.

Papaya: Papaya is known as the medical melon of the tropics. It is rich in vitamin C. It is a fair source of vitamin A and iron. It possesses an enzyme papain which has the same digestive effect as pepsin. It also contains fibrin. This is an element which is valuable in clotting blood and is rarely found except in humans and animals. Iron and phosphorus of papaya are easily digested and assimilated.

Raw papaya is good for liver troubles, including jaundice.

Raw Banana: Like the jackfruit and papaya, banana is used as a fruit when ripe and as a vegetable in its unripe state. And like the coconut, each part of the fruit and tree are used. It equals potato in nutritive values. It contains starch, minerals and vitamins in high portions.

Banana is rich in solids–potassium, phosphorus, sulphur, calcium, magnesium, iron, copper and iodine. It has sugar which the body quickly assimilates and is used as energy. Its soluble fibres helps in lowering cholesterol.

Potato: The world production of potato exceeds even that of wheat.

Potato is rich in vitamin C and B_6. It is high in potassium, phosphorus, magnesium, iron, copper, fibre and also in carbohydrates. Its potassium content is higher than that of oranges. It protein content is of high value and has 9 different amino acids of importance. It is highly alkaline with salts rich in soda and potash, but low in lime. But its vitamin C content reduces sharply with storage.

Freshly harvested potatoes are comparatively richer in other nutrients also.

Lady Fingers: It is rich in sulphur, chlorine and vitamin C and fair in iron and potassium. It is alkaline in effect. It contains a large amount of pectose. The pectose jellies when cooked in water. This jelly aids the enzyme action for assimilation of foods.

Radish: Radish is quite unique in the sense that it is the only vegetable which is at the same time saline, bitter, warm, sweet pungent and cool. It is light to digest, appetising, stimulant of gastric fire, and good for the heart. It cures asthma, cough, gas troubles, piles, liver and kidney problems. This is the only vegetable which has a substantial amount of arsenic and is, therefore, beneficial for thyroid glands. Juice of radish and its leaves are extremely good if taken during jaundice.

Brinjal: Also known as aubergines or eggplants, brinjals vary in shape from the large and spherical to the elongated and berry-like and is either purple or white in colour. Among the first vegetables to be used by Ayurvedic doctors, the brinjal was prescribed as a heat tonic, an appetite stimulant, a mild laxative and diuretic.

Recent clinical tests have shown the brinjal is anticarcinogenic, anticonvulsant and valuable in reducing cholesterol.

Mustard: Mustard greens are the richest known source of dietary lime. They are also high in vitamins A and C and in dietary iron and calcium. It strengthens heart muscles, prevents hairfall and helps in stomach troubles. Its extract is a digestant and an agreeable spice. Addition of mustard to a hot bath, when one is thoroughly frozen, is a good cure.

Parsley: Parsley has a strong flavour and mild taste, used for flavouring and garnishing. A reputed mouth freshener; chewed after garlic, onion and alcohol, it freshens the breath. It is a good source of chlorophyll, organic iron, calcium, phosphorus, manganese and vitamin A, B and C. These nutrients make parsley useful in anaemia, congested liver and asthma.

Peas: Peas are rich in soluble fibre and also has iron, phosphorus, sulphur, chlorine and vitamin B. They help rescue LDL cholesterol and also blood sugar.

Spinach: Spinach is the foremost among the chlorophyle group of vegetables. Its extremely rich in vitamins A and E, iron, potassium, sulphur and chlorine and fair in vitamin B and C and calcium. Spinach can be easily digested. It is beneficial for most patients. It is a good purgative and hence helpful in constipation. Since it is rich in vitamin A, it promotes eyesight. The chewing of raw spinach cures pyorrhoea. Its regular use helps to prevent the deficiency of folic acid. In all, spinach contributes roughage, colour and is a low calorie filler which makes for a balanced meal.

Tamarind: A sour fruit, used extensively in India, tamarind was actually native to Africa. The pulp, leaves, seeds and bark are all beneficial. The ripened tamarind fruit helps to quench thirst because the pulp consists of moisture. The pulp also contains tartaric acid and pectin in good quantities. The leaves are cooling and antibilious and the fruit pulp is digestive, cooling, acts as a laxative and antiseptic and is rich in vitamin C. Tamarind is used to treat bronchial disorders and gargling with tamarind water is recommended for a sore throat.

Tomatoes: According to the Ayurvedas, the tomato is light, juicy, warm, a stimulant, an appetizer, a laxative, anti-flatulent and helps abate cough. The tomato is a rich source of vitamin A. It is remarkable that its vitamin C content is not destroyed easily. It is an excellent source of iron and a good provider of phosphorus, calcium, potassium, sulphur, magnesium, chlorine, sodium, and iodine.

Unlike other vegetables, tomatoes have very little carbohydrate and hence are good for diabetic patients and for those who are trying to shed weight. It is good in all cases of anaemia. It strengthens the teeth and gums.

GLOSSARY

FOODGRAINS

English	Spiked millet	Barley	Jowar	Italian millet	Maize (dry)	Oatmeal	Ragi
Hindi	Bajra	Jau	Juar-janera	Kangri	Makai	Jai	Okra
Tamil	Cambu	Barli arisi	Cholam	Thenai	Muka cholam	—	Ragi
Telugu	Gantelu	Barli biyyam	Jonnalu	Korralu	Mekka jonnalu	—	Chollu
Marathi	Bajri	Juv	Jwari	Rala	Muka	—	Nachni
Bengali	Bajra	Job	Juar	Syamadhan kangni	Sukna paka bhutta	Jai	—
Gujarati	Bajri	Jau	Juar	Ral kang	Makai	—	Ragi bhav
Malayalam	Kamboo	Yavam	Cholam	Thina	Unakku cholam	Oat mavu	Moothari (korra)
Kannada	—	—	Jola	—	Vonugida musikinu	Jolu	Ragi
Kashmiri	Baajr'u	Wushku	—	Shol	Makka'y	—	—

Contd...

Foodstuff	Rice (raw)	Rice (parboiled)	Rice (white)	Rice (black)	Rice flakes	Rice (puffed)	Samai
Hindi	Arwa chawal	Usna chawal	Safed chaval	Chaval (kala)	Chowla	Murmura	Kutki, Sanwali
Tamil	Pachai arisi	Puzhungal arisi	Vellai puttu arisi	Karuppu puttu arisi	Arisi aval	Arisia pori	Samai
Telugu	Pachi biyyam	Uppudu biyyam	Thella biyyam	Nalla biyyam	Atukulu	Murmuralu	—
Marathi	Tandool	Tandool ukda	—	—	Pohe	Murmure	Sava
Bengali	Atap chowl	Siddha chowl	—	—	Chaler khood	Muri	Kangni
Gujarati	Hatna	Ukadelloo chokha	—	—	Pohva	Mumra	—
Maiayalam	Pacchari	Puzhungal ari	Velutha puttari	Karutha puttari	Avil	Pori	—
Kannada	Kotnuda	Kotnuda	—	—	Avalukki	—	Puri
Kashmiri	—	—	—	—	—	—	—

Contd...

English	Semolina	Vermicelli	Wheat (whole)	Wheat flour (whole)	Wheat flour (refined)	Wheat (broken)
Hindi	Sooji	Siwain	Gehun	Atta	Maida	Daliya
Tamil	Ravai	Semiya	Godumai	Muzhu godmai ma	Maida mavu	Godhumbi ravai
Telugu	Rawa	Semiya	Godhumalu	Godhum pindi	Maidha pindi	Dinchina gadhumalu
Marathi	—	Shevaya	Gahu	Gahu kuneek	Gahu kuneek	Gavache satva
Bengali	Suji	Sewai	Gomasta	Atta	Maida	Bhanga gom
Gujarati	—	—	Ghau	Ato	—	Fadia ghaun
Malayalam	Rava	Semiya	Muzhu gothambu	Gothambu mavu	Maidu tha gothambu mavu	Gothumbu ari
Kannada	—	Shavige	Godhi	Godhi	Hittu madia	Kuttida Godhi
Kashmiri	—	Ku' nu'	—	—	—	—

VEGETABLES

English	Ash gourd	Bitter gourd	Bottle gourd	Brinjal	Broad beans	Cabbage	Capsicum
Hindi	Safed petha	Karela	Ghia	Baingan	Sem	Bandhgobi	Simla mirch
Bengali	Chal kumdo	karala	Laoo	Begoon	Sheem	Badha kopee	Lonka
Assamese	Lao bishesh	—	Jati lao	Bengena	Urahi	Bondhakobi	Kashmiri jalakai
Oriya	Pani kakkaru	—	Lau	Baigana	Shimba	Patrokobi	Simla lonka
Marathi	Kohala	Karle	Dudhi	Wangi	Ghewda	Pan kobi	Bhopli mirchi
Gujarati	Petha	Karela	Dudhi	Ringna	Papdi	Kobi	Simla marchan
Telugu	Boodie gumadi	Kakara	Sorakaya	Vankaya	Pedda chikkudu	Kosu	Pedda mirappa
Kannada	Budu gumbala	Hagalkai	Sorekai	Badanekai	Chapparadavare	Kosu	Donne menasinakai
Tamil	Pooshanikkai	Pavakkai	Suraikai	Kaththarikai	Avaraikai	Muttaikosu	Kuda milakai
Malayalam	Kumbalanga	Kaypakka	Cheraikai	Vazhutheninga	Amarakai	Muttakose	Parangi mulagu
Kashmiri	Masha'ly al	Karelu	—	Waangun	—	Bandgobhi	—

Contd...

English	Carrot	Cauliflower	Cluster beans	Colocasia	Coriander leaves	Cucumber	Curry leaves
Hindi	Gajar	Phulgobi	Guar ki phalli	Arvi	Hara Dhania	Khira	Kadi patta
Bengali	Gujar	Foolcopy	Jhar sim	—	Dhonay pata	Sasha	Curry pata
Assamese	Gajor	Phoolkobi	—	Kochu	Dhania paat	—	Narasingha paat
Oriya	Gajar	Phulakobi	—	—	Dhania patra	—	Bhrusanga patta
Marathi	Gajar	Fulkobi	Govari	Alu kanda	Kothimbir	Kakari	Kadhi patta
Gujarati	Gajar	Fool kobi	Govar	Alvi	Kothmir	Kakdi	Mitho limdo
Telugu	Gajjara	Cauliflower	Goruchikkudu kayalu	Chamadumpa	Kothimeera	Dosakaya	Karivepaku
Kannada	Gajjari	Hookosu	Gorikayi	Keshave	Kottambari soppu	Southaikayi	Karibevu
Tamil	Carrot	Koveppu	Kothavarangai	Seppann kizhangu	Koththamali ilaigal	Kakkarikkai	Kariveppilai
Malayalam	Carrot	Coliflower	Kothavara	Chembu	Kothamalli ila	Vellari	Kariveppila
Kashmiri	—	Phoolgobhi	—	—	—	Laa'r	—

Contd...

English	Drumstick	French beans	Garlic	Ginger (fresh)	Green chillies	Jackfruit	Lady's finger
Hindi	Sahjan ki phali	Pharsbeen	Lassan	Adrak	Hari mirch	Kathal	Bhindi
Bengali	Sajane dauta	French beans	Rasoon	Ada (tatka)	Kancha lonka	Echore	Dhanroce
Assamese	Sajina	Faras been	Naharoo	Ada (kesa)	Kesa jalakia	—	Bhendi
Oriya	Sajana chhuin	French beans	Rasuna	Ada (kancha)	Kancha lonka	—	Bhendi
Marathi	Shevgyachya shenga	Farasbi	Lasun	Aale	Hirvya mirchya	Kawla phanas	Bhendi
Gujarati	Saragvani shing	Fansi	Lasan	Adu	Lila marcha	Phunas	Bhinda
Telugu	Munagakayalu	French chikkudu	Vellulli	Allam (pachchi)	Pachchi mirapakayalu	Letha panasa	Bendakaaya
Kannada	Nuggekai	Avare	Bellulli	Ashi Shunti	Hasi menasinakai	Yele halasu	Bendekai
Tamil	Murungaikai	Beans	Ulli Poondu	Inji	Pachchai milagai	Pila pinchu	Vendaikai
Malayalam	Muringakkaya	Beans	Veluthulli	Inji	Pachamulagu	Idichakka	Vendakka
Kashmiri	—	—	Ruhan	—	Myool martsu waungun	—	Bindu

Contd...

English	Lettuce	Lemon	Mint leaves	Onion	Parwal	Peas	Plantain flower	Plantain green
Hindi	Salad ke patte	Nimbu	Pudina	Pyaz	Parwal	Matar	Kele ka phool	Kacha kela
Bengali	Lettuce	Lebu	Poodina pata	Pyaz	Potol	Motor	Mocha	Kancha kala
Assamese	Laipaat	Nemu	Podina	—	Patol	Motormah	—	—
Oriya	Lettuce	Lembu	Podana patra	—	Potala	Matar	—	—
Marathi	Saladchi paane	Limbu	Pudina	Kanda	—	Matar	Kel phool	Kele
Gujarati	Lettuce	Limbu	Fudino	Dungli	—	Vatana	Kelphool	Kela
Telugu	Lettuce koora	Nimma	Pudhina koora	Nirulli	—	Bathanedu	Aratipuwu	Arati kayi
Kannada	Lettuce soppu	Nimbu	Pudina sopu	Erulli	—	Betani	Balo mothu	Bala kayi
Tamil	Lettuce keerai	Elumicham pazham	Pudhinaa	Vengayam	—	Pattani	Vazhaippu	Vazhaikkai
Malayalam	Uvarcheera	Cherunaranga	Pudhinaa	Ulli	—	Pattani Payaru	Vazhappoo	Vazhakka
Kashmiri	Salaad	—	—	Gandu	—	Matar	—	—

Contd...

English	Plantain stem	Potato	Radish	Red pumpkin	Ridge gourd	Snake gourd	Sweet potato	Yam elephant
Hindi	Kele ka tana	Aloo	Muli	Sitaphal	Torai	—	Shakarkand	Zaminkand
Bengali	Thor	Aloo	Mulo	Ronga Koomra	Jhinge	Chichinga	Rangalu	Kham aloo
Assamese	—	Alu	—	Ronga lao	—	—	—	Kaath aloo
Oriya	—	Alu	—	Kakharu	—	—	—	Deshi alu
Marathi	Kelecha khunt	Batate	Mula	Lal bhopla	Dodka	Pudwal	Ratale	Suran
Gujarati	Kelanu thed	Batata	Mula	Kolu	Turai	Pandola	Sakkaria	Suran
Telugu	Arati davva	Bangaala dumpa	Mullangi	Erra gummadi	Beerakai	Potlakayi	Dumpalu	Kanda dumpa
Kannada	Dindu	Aalugadde	Mullangi	Kempu kumbala	Heeraikai	Padavalai	Genasu	Suvarnagadde
Tamil	Vazhaithandu	Urulaikizhangu	Mullangi	Parangikai	Pirrkkankai	Podalangai	Sarkarai valli kizhangu	Chenai kizhangu
Malayalam	Vazhappindi	Uralakkizhangu	Mullangi	Chuvappu mathan	Pecchinga	Padavalanga	Chakkara kizhangu	Chena
Kashmiri	—	Oloo	Muj	Paarimal	Turrelu	—	—	—

PULSES

English	Bengal gram (whole)	Bengal gram (split)	Black gram (split)	Black gram (whole)	Cornflour	Cow gram`	Green gram (whole)
Hindi	Chana	Chana dal	Urad dal	Sabat urad	Makai ka atta	Lobia (bada)	Moong
Bengali	Chola	Banglar chhola	Mashkolair dal	Mashkolai dal	Bhoottar maida	Barbati	Mug
Assamese	—	Buttor dail	Matir dail (phola)	Matir dail (gota)	Moida	—	—
Oriya	—	Buta (chhota)	Biri (phala)	Biri (gota)	Makka atta	—	—
Marathi	Hurbhura	Chana dal	Udid dal	Udid	Makyache pith	Kuleeth	Mug
Gujarati	Chana	Chana nidaal	Adad ni dal	Adad	Makai no lot	—	Mag
Telugu	Sanagalu	Senaga pappu	Mina pappu	Minu mulu	Mokkajonnalu (pindi)	Ada chandalu	Pesalu
Kannada	Kadale	Kadale bela	Uddina bela	Uddu	Musukinajolada hittu	Thadaguni	Hesaru kalu
Tamil	Muzhu kadalai	Kadalai paruppu	Ulutham paruppu	Ulundhu	Chola Maavu	Karamani	Pachai payaru
Malayalam	Kadala	Kadala parippu	Uzhunnu parrippu	Uzhunnu	Cholapodi	Payar	Cherupayaru
Kashmiri	Chanu	—	Maha	—	—	—	Muang

Contd...

English	Green gram (split)	Horse gram	Kesari dal	Kidney beans	Red gram	Red lentils	Soya bean
Hindi	Moong dal	Kulthi	Lang dal	Rajma	Arhar dal	Masoor dal	Bhat
Bengali	—	Kulthi kalai	Khesari	Barbati beej	Arhar dal	Lal masoor (bhanga)	Gari kalai
Assamese	—	—	—	Markhowa urahi	Rahor dail	Masoor dail (phola)	—
Oriya	—	—	—	Baragudi chhuin	Harada dali	Masura dali (phala)	—
Marathi	—	Kuleeth	Lakh dal	—	Tur dal	Masur dal	Soya
Gujarati	—	Kuleeth	Lakh	—	Tuver dal	Masur dal	Soya
Telugu	Pesaru pappu	Ulavalu	Lamka pappu	—	Kandi pappu	Missu pappu	—
Kannada	Hesare bele	Huruli	—	—	Togar bele	Masur bele	—
Tamil	Pasi paruppu	Kollu	Vattuparuppu	—	Thuvaram parappu	Massor paruppu	—
Malayalam	Cherupayar parippu	Muthira	—	—	Thuvara parippu	Masoor parippu	Soya bean
Kashmiri	—	—	—	—	—	Musur	—

FRUITS AND DRY FRUITS

English	Almond	Coconut	Currants	Dates	Dry plums
Hindi	Badam	Nariyal	Mungaqqa	Khajur	Alu bukhara
Bengali	Badam	Narcole	Manaca	Khejoor	Sookno kool
Assamese	Badam	Narikol	Kismis	Khejur	Sukan bogori
Oriya	Badaam	Nadia	Kala kismis	Khajura	Barakoli jateeya phala
Marathi	Badam	Naral	Manuka	Khajur	Alubhukar
Gujarati	Badam	Naliyer	Kalli draksh	Khajoor	Suka Plum
Telugu	Badam	Kobbari kaaya	Endu nalla dhraksha	Kharjoora pandu	—
Kannada	Badami	Tenginakai	Dweepa dharakshi-kappu	Kharjoora	—
Tamil	Badam/vadhumai	Thengai	Karumdhraakshai	Perichampazham	Aalpacota ular pazham
Malayalam	Badam	Nalikeram/Thenga	Karuthamurthiri	Eethapazham	—

Contd...

English	Guavas	Lemon	Orange	Raisins	Walnuts
Hindi	Amrud	Nimbu	Santra	Kishmish	Akhrot
Bengali	Payara	Lebu	Kamla lebu	Kishmish	Akhrot
Assamese	Madhurium	Nemu	Sumothira	Sukan angoor	Akhrot
Oriya	Pijuli	Lembu	Kamala	Kismis	Akhrot
Marathi	Peru	Limbu	Santre	Bedane	Akrod
Gujarati	Jamrukh	Limbu	Santara	Lal draksh	Akhrot
Telugu	Jaamapandu	Nimma	Kamala Pandu	Kismis pallu	Aakrot
Kannada	Seebe	Nimbe	Kittale	Dweepadrakshi	Acrota
Tamil	Koyyapazham	Elumicham pazham	Kichilipazham	Ular dhraakshai	Akhrot
Malayalam	Perakkai	Cherunaranga	Madhura naranga	Unakkamunthiri	Akrotandi

Dry Spices

English	Aniseed	Asafoetida	Basil leaves	Bay leaf	Caraway seeds	Cardamom (brown)	Cardamom (green)	Cinnamon
Hindi	Saunf	Hing	Tulse ke patte	Tej patta	Shahjeera	Moti elaichi	Choti elaichi	Dalchini
Bengali	Mowri	Hing	Tulsi pata	Tej pata	Sajeera	Elach (tamate)	Elach (sobooj)	Daroochini
Assamese	Guwamori	Hing	Tulosi paat	Tejpaat	Bilati jira	Ilachi (muga)	Ilachi (sevjia)	Dalcheni
Oriya	·Panamahuri	Hengu	Tulasi patra	Teja patra	Sahajira	Aleicha	Gijuratie	Dalachini
Marathi	Badishep	Hing	Tulsichi paney	Tamal patra	Shahjeera	Masala welchi	Welchi (hirvi)	Dalchini
Gujarati	Variyali	Hing	Tulsina pan	Tamal patra	Jiru	Elcho	Lila alchi	Tuj
Telugu	Sopaginja	Inguva	Thulasi akulu	—	Seema sopyginjale	Yalakulu	Yala kulu (pachavi)	Dalchina chekka
Kannada	Sopubeeja	Hingu	Tulasi ele	—	Caraway beejagalre	Yalakki	Yalakki (hasuru)	Dalchini
Tamil	Perumjeerakam	Perungaayam	Thulasi	—	Karunjeerakam	Elakkai (Pazhuppu)	Elakkai (pachchai)	Lavangapattai
Malayalam	Perumjeerakam	Kaayam	Tulasi	—	Karunjeerakam	Elakkaya	Pach Elakkaya	Karuvapatta
Kashmiri	—	Yangu	—	—	—	Aal budu'a aal	—	—

Contd...

English	Cloves	Coriander seeds	Cumin seeds	Fenugreek seeds	Mace	Mustard seeds	Nutmeg	Parsley
Hindi	Laung	Sukha dhania	Jeera	Methi dana	Javitri	Rai	Jaiphal	Ajmooda ka patta
Bengali	Labango	Dhonay	Jeera	Methi	Jaeetri	Sarsay	Jaifall	Parsley
Assamese	Long	Dhania guti	Gota jeera	Paleng	Janee	Sarioh guti	Jaaiphal-	Sugandhi lota
Oriya	Labanga	Dhania	Jira	Methi	Jayatree	Sorisha	Jaiphala	Balabalua shaga
Marathi	Lavanga	Dhane	Jire	Methi dane	Jaypatri	Mohari	Jayphal	Ajmoda
Gujarati	Laving	Dhana	Jeeru	Methi	Jaypatra	Rai	Jaypal	Ajmo
Telugu	Lavangalu	Dhaniyalu	Jeelakara	Menthulu	Japathri	Aavaalu	Jaikaaya	Kothimeerajati koora
Kannada	Lavanga	Kottambari beeja	Jeerige	Menthe	Japatri	Sasive kalu	Jaika	Kottambari jotiya soppu
Tamil	Kraambu	Koththamali virai	Jeerakam	Vendhayam	Jaadipathri	Kadugu	Jaadhikai	Kothamalu ilaigal pole
Malayalam	Karayaamboovu	Kothamalli	Jeerakam	Uluva	Jathipathri	Kadugu	Jathikka	Malliela pole
Kashmiri	Ru'ang	Daaniwal	Zyur	—	Jalwatur	—	Zaaphal	

Contd...

English	Peppercorns	Pomegranate seeds	Poppy seeds	Red Chillies	Tamarind	Turmeric	Vinegar	Thymol
Hindi	Kali mirch ke daane	Anardana	Khus khus	Lal mirch	Imli	Haldi	Sirka	Ajwain
Bengali	Marich	Dareem bij	Posto	Paka lonka	Tentool	Halood	Seerka	—
Assamese	Jaluk	Dalim guti	—	Sukan jalakia	Teteli	Halodhi	Sirika	—
Oriya	Golamaricha	Dalimba manji	—	Nali lankamaricha	Tentuli	Haladi	Vinegar	—
Marathi	Kale Miri	Dalimbache dane	Khas khas	Lal mirchya	Chincha	Halad	Sirka	Onva
Gujarati	Mari	Dadamna bee	Khaskhas	Lal marcha	Amli	Haldar	Sirko	—
Telugu	Miriyaalu	Daanimma ginjalu	Gasagasaalu	Erra mirapa kayalu	Chinthapandu	Pasupu	—	—
Kannada	Menasina kalu	Dalimbo beeja	Gasagase beeja	Kempu menasinakai	Hunase hannu	Arasina	—	—
Tamil	Milagu	Maadhulai vidhai	Kasakasaa	Milagai vatal	Puli	Manjal	Pulikaadi	—
Malayalam	Kurumulagu	Madhala naranga kuru	Kaskas	Chuvanna Mulagu	Puli	Manjal	Vinagiri	—

Rice Bonanza

—Manjira Majumdar

50 novel rice dishes from Kashmir to Kerala

Rice, a complete food in itself, mirrors India's culinary diversity binding us as a people of a single nation. For the first time this unique and outstanding book takes you on a culinary adventure through the kitchens of India giving you a vast array of lip-smacking rice dishes culled from all parts of our country.

• Yakhni Pulao of Kashmir • Tehri of Punjab • Jeera Rice of Delhi • Meat Pulao of Uttar Pradesh • Fish Kofta Pulao of Bengal • Ven Pongal of Tamil Nadu • Kochi Seafood Pulao of Kerala • Vangi Bhaat of Maharashtra ...and many types of desserts

...go ahead, enjoy eating mouth-watering delicacies to your heart's content.

Price: Rs. 125/- • Pages: 144 (colour) Postage: Rs. 15/-

Paneer Bonanza

—Prabhjot Mundhir

New exotic and mouth-watering paneer dishes for all occasions.

55

STARTERS • SOUPS

GEGGIES • SALADS

PIZZAS • SNACKS

DESSERTS

An invaluable treasury of traditional, yet novel recipes of *Paneer* distilled over 50 years of culinary knowledge and expertise.

- Easy to prepare.
- Teaches simple touches with everyday vegetables to make them special.
- Phenomenal range.

Delicious and nutritious too!

Price: Rs. 96/- • Pages: 158 + 16 (Colour) • Postage: Rs. 15/-

Over 100 Fat-Free Recipes

—Elizabeth Jyothi Mathew

With fast food and junk food being the order of the day, thanks to our rushed modern existence, staying healthy is of prime importance. More often than not, we forego some of the most delicious food in order to stay healthy. It is not necessary to give up culinary delicacies to maintain good health. This book shows just how.

The author discloses dishes that are nutritious as well as low in calories and high on taste. This book takes readers on a journey of culinary experimentation with different recipes that can then be incorporated into a healthy lifestyle. The recipes are divided into four sections: Vegetable Dishes, Meat and Poultry Dishes, Seafood Dishes and Desserts. These calorie-counted recipes will help you maintain a diet that includes various types of food, ensuring all your nutritional requirements are met. So, eat well and stay slim and healthy with ***Over 100 Fat-free Recipes***.

Demy Size • Pages: 120
Price: Rs. 80/- • Postage: Rs. 15/-

Cooking for Diabetics

—Satarupa Banerjee

Diet plays a very important role for any disease, more so for diabetes

There was a time when diabetic diet meant uninspiring tasteless food. Thankfully the diet scene for the diabetics is no longer gloomy or bland as it used to be.

Within a few restrictions, diabetic food is definitely a gourmet fare now. This book will show how diabetic food can not only benefit the patient but lead the way for a healthy lifestyle that the whole family will benefit from.

Demy Size • Pages: 115
Price: Rs. 96/- • Postage: 15/-

Bread Bonanza

—Sangeeta Gupta

Bake Fresh & Nutritious Continental Bread at Home

Are you sick and tired of eating breads from the market? Do you crave for fresh and nutritious loaf of bread taken out directly from the oven on your breakfast table? Then baking at home is a healthy idea. Whether you're apprehensively curious or an ambitious beginner, *BREAD BONANZA* will help you rise to the challenge of baking delicious breads that turn out perfect every time. Continental breads can be made easily like the Indian flat breads.

BREAD BONANZA is the first of its kind in India that explains you from basics: every succinct description of the techniques with illustrations. Every lesson will clear your doubts and lead you further to master the most common types of bread: batter bread, egg bread, white bread, whole wheat bread, holiday sweet bread, flat bread, and coffee cake.

This book's contemporary approach shows you the way to make homemade breads faster and easier than ever before.

Price: Rs. 125/- • Pages: 152 (colour)
Postage: Rs. 20/-

Nutritious Mushroom Recipes

—Prabhjot Mundhir

'Foods can make or break you' is an established fact. That is why it is important to include the mushroom – one of nature's greatest wonder foods – in one's diet. The common variety is full of high quality protein as well as B vitamins. With its irresistible taste, exotic flavour and rich aroma, the mushroom's delicious dishes are a healthy alternative to meat dishes. Keeping Indian tastes in mind, the author has innovated some easy-to-follow recipes.

The book contains recipes on starters, soups, salads and dishes for the main course. Some of the starters and quick stir-fried vegetable dishes of mushrooms are just ideal for tiffin boxes of children, working women and other office-goers. Most ingredients used are easily available. These dishes can easily be a part of any Indian or Continental menu set for special occasions too. In short, mushrooms used in everyday cooking will help maintain the good health of your loved ones.

Price: Rs. 125/- • Pages: 128 (colour)
Postage: Rs. 15/-

Dishes and Desserts

—Tanushree Podder

Wide range of delicious vegetarian and non-vegetarian dishes and desserts

As the process of globalisation is gaining momentum, people are turning more adventurous and sampling the culture, cuisine and art of different states, countries and people. No longer are people confined to their culture and cuisine.

No longer is 'dosa' or 'idli', a south Indian preserve. It has broken the barriers and travelled all over the world. So have 'rasgulla' and 'tandoori chicken'! They have become immensely popular among the masses.

It is a secret dream of every woman to be appreciated for her cooking and to spread a sumptuous fare for her family. This book is written for every woman who wants to be a proud cook. The simple language and elaborate instructions make it easy to follow the recipes. Now you can churn out those fantastic dishes at home, which you could earlier eat only at restaurants and hotels.

Pages: 172 • Price: Rs. 96/- (colour)• Postage: Rs. 15/-

Microwave Cooking...made easy

—Prabhjot Mundhir

Innovative, yet traditional Veg & Non-veg dishes – Indian, Continental, Chinese and Italian Cuisine

Why microwave food?

• It's faster • It's tastier • It's nutritious • It's Convenient • It's economical

Do you think a microwave oven's main function is to reheat leftovers? Well, think again. As a matter of fact, there is so much more you can do with it. You can easily make dishes like sarson-ka-saag, chicken tikka and momos in a jiffy, bake a cake or a pizza in minutes. Cook anything, anytime.

This small book covers:

• Useful & interesting tips
• Do's & don'ts of microwave cooking
• Facts about microwave & its working
• And much more... in the simplest way possible!

Also over 100 delicious recipes for—

• Basic Pastes • Sauces • Soups • Salads • Snacks
• Breakfast • Relishes • Desserts • Main Course dishes

Enjoy healthy meals with your family and friends.

Pages: 160 • Price: Rs. 125/- (colour) • Postage: Rs. 15/-

Corn Cuisine

—Prabhjot Mundhir

Corn — the very mention of the word conjures up visions of hot, tasty, freshly roasted, golden corn cobs relished with gusto during the summer and rainy season. But there is much more than just that. A versatile grain, it can be boiled, ground, grilled, roasted and cooked in numerous ways. An array of exotic dishes can be experimented and enjoyed.

Make Mexican Tacos, Italian Polenta, Chinese Chicken-Corn Soup, American Corn Bread, Methauries, and other fancy veg and non-veg dishes. These mouth-watering delicious treats can easily be prepared at home. Sure to tickle your taste buds and satisfy your palate!

Surprise your guests. Let them wonder at your expertise in making every corn recipe they can think of. Known for its high fibre and carbohydrate content, it is a boon for the health-conscious too. 60 corn recipes for all occasions, a bonanza for all corn lovers!

Pages: 148 • Price: Rs. 125/- (colour) • Postage: Rs. 15/-

Books on Housekeeping Relationship & Beauty

150/-

80/-

96/-

150/-

96/-

Be Your Own Beautician

—Parvesh Handa

A guide for a health conscious woman and for a professional as well. Learn and practise complete body & beauty care at home

Those blessed with healthy skin, attractive features, youthful charm and glamorous body are fortunate. This book will tell you exactly how to make and present the best of yourself, how to look radiant from head to feet with the help of natural beauty aids and herbal ingredients. This book describes useful tips for both men and women, in detail, to bring out your beauty and explains various questions to the readers:

- If you have chosen the right cosmetics to bring out your beauty?
- How to shape your face, eyes and lips to look their loveliest?
- If you know how to give your type of skin lasting attraction?
- If your hair is alluring and does your hairstyle enhance your personality?
- If you know the secrets of successful figure control?

The author of this book has the honour to write the first book on herbal beauty care published in India in 1982.

Big Size • Pages: 160
Price: Rs. 120/- • Postage: Rs. 15/-

Smart Housekeeping
for the woman of today

—Rupa Chatterjee

A housewife is very often judged by the way she keeps her house. For her it's like a temple – a key through which she can ensure highest level of physical and emotional comfort for her family.

And in view of its critical significance in one's life, it's imperative that your home is managed well – an art every homemaker needs to master.

This book, written by a seasoned housewife who is also a professional interior designer, is one such handy help that deals with the subject in a critical and comprehensive manner. Never before have so many tips and suggestions, covering every aspect of the subject, been put together in a single volume. From interior decoration, time management, organising household chores, cleaning of house and its security, maintaining of gadgets and household articles to household budget, etiquette for all occasions, first aid, travel and transfer, personal grooming, it goes on to cover tips on energy conservation and interpersonal relationships.

A must for all who wish to make their home a paradise.

Big Size • Pages: 296
Price: Rs. 150/- • Postage: 20/-